# MOHANDAS GANDHI

# GLENN ALAN CHENEY

# MOHANDAS GANDHI

FRANKLIN WATTS
NEW YORK | LONDON | TORONTO | SYDNEY | 1983
AN IMPACT BIOGRAPHY

A GROLIER COMPANY

Cover photograph courtesy of United Press International

Photographs courtesy of:
Information Service of India: pp. 15, 34, and 97;
United Press International: pp. 53, 78, 80, and 92;
The Bettmann Archive, Inc.: pp. 74, 81, and 91.

Library of Congress Cataloging in Publication Data

Cheney, Glenn Alan.
Mohandas Gandhi.

(An Impact biography)
Includes bibliographical references and index.
Summary: Describes briefly the colonial India into
which Gandhi was born, his upbringing and education,
including his stay in South Africa, and the nonviolent
revolution he led to free India from English rule.
1. Gandhi, Mahatma, 1869–1948. 2. Statesmen—India—Biography.
[1. Gandhi, Mahatma, 1869–1948. 2. Statesmen.
3. India—History—British occupation, 1765–1947] I. Title.
DS481.G3C487  1983    954.03′5′0924    [B]    [92]    82-24848
ISBN 0-531-04600-1

# CONTENTS

TO RAYMUNDA
DA SILVA LESSA

# MOHANDAS GANDHI

# THE MAHATMA'S INDIA

## 1

"My mission is not merely the brotherhood of Indian humanity. My mission is not merely the freedom of India. . . . But through the realization of the freedom of India, I hope to realize and carry on the mission of the brotherhood of man."

You could call it a revolutionary revolution. Such a strategy was unimaginably absurd. An army of a quarter of a billion men, women, and children passively offered themselves for imprisonment, impoverishment, and slaughter. Their leader held neither government office nor military rank. At the height of his strength, he weighed 110 pounds (50 kg). His only armor was a loincloth of homespun cotton; his only weapon an undefinable but undeniable Truth. This man, his Truth, and his pacifist army waged a war of nonviolent resistance against the largest empire in the world. And they won.

## THE MAN

The man was Mahatma Gandhi. He called himself "a Christian, a Hindu, a Moslem, and a Jew." British military leader Louis Mountbatten, the last viceroy of India, said he would go down in history "on a par with Buddha and Jesus Christ." Physicist Albert Einstein said that "generations to come will scarce believe that such a one as this ever in flesh and blood walked upon this earth." American General George C. Marshall called him "the spokesman for the conscience of all mankind." British playwright George Bernard Shaw said he was "not a man, he was a phenomenon."

He owned nothing but homemade clothes, a pair of eyeglasses, and a watch. He slept outdoors on the ground without complaint. His diet would have barely sustained a child. When his conscience demanded it, he offered his life to his people or to his adversaries by fasting until they, too, heard the "inner voice" that revealed what was right and what was wrong.

Gandhi was born in India, educated in England, inspired in South Africa, and driven beyond mortal expectations while working to improve conditions in his Indian homeland. He defied the traditions, rules, and mores of his society and disregarded the laws of the British Empire. He did this for neither power nor profit. Never, except once in his childhood, did he ignore his conscience or forget the ultimate Truth that he respected more than his life.


HIS COUNTRY

India is one of the oldest civilizations in the world. Its identity as classical India dates back to 1500 B.C. Until relatively recently, India's government was not centralized. Hundreds of semi-autonomous principalities jealously guarded their territories and subcultures. Even today, India has some fifteen different languages. Indians from different areas must converse in the official languages of Hindi or English.

The Indian culture also includes several distinctly different religions. The Aryan invasion of 1500 B.C. brought the myths, rituals, philosophies, and sacred writings of the *Veda*, which includes the sacred texts of the *Upanishads* and the *Bhagavad Gita*. Together with the various pagan religions of India, the *Veda* became the foundation of Hinduism.

Beginning in the ninth century A.D., the Moslem (or

Islamic) religion arrived via invasions by Turkey and Afghanistan, which were part of the Mogul Empire. Much more aggressive than the religiously passive Hindus, the Moslems held political control over India. Although many Hindus converted to Islam, by 1869, when Gandhi was born, only a quarter of the population was Moslem. The Christian, Buddhist, and Sikh religions comprised about 5 percent of the population, with the Hindus an approximate 70 percent majority.

The Hindu religion does not have the ordered and organizational structure of the Christian, Jewish, and Moslem religions. Myriad sects and subsects hold different beliefs and pray to different gods. Among the beliefs held in common are reincarnation, or the rebirth of the soul in a different body, and the upward development of the soul as each incarnation improves itself through prayer, purity, and good behavior.

One striking characteristic of Hinduism pervades India — the caste system. There are four castes, each of which is divided into several subcastes. Castes are much more rigidly separated than the social classes of other countries. Marriage between different castes is strongly discouraged, and in the past was prohibited, so all Hindus are born into the caste of their parents. The Brahmins are the highest and most respected caste. Said to be related to ancient holy priests, the Brahmins oversee holy temples where marriages, funerals, and other rituals are performed. Below the Brahmins are the Kshatriyas, the noble class related to the former ruling princes. Third are the Vaisya, the large middle class of merchants, cattle breeders, government officials, and others in commercial and agricultural occupations. Gandhi's caste was Vaisya. Lowest of all are the Sudras, who are supposedly descended from slaves.

The people of the lowest Sudra subcaste are the Untouchables, the poorest and most disrespected of all Indians. In Gandhi's time, to touch them or even cross their shadows meant spiritual and physical pollution. If an Untouchable drank from a well reserved for casted Hindus, its water was forever tainted. Until recently, Untouchables were banned from temples and schools. The only work they were permitted was cleaning latrines, sweeping streets, and other jobs that no one else would do. Mahatma Gandhi was the first person in Indian history to respect the Untouchables. He went so far as to love them as brothers and sisters.

No one seriously fought to change the caste system until Gandhi. Even the Untouchables accepted their position as part of their fate. There were hundreds of subcastes, and every Indian was born into a certain predestined position in society. Everything from one's profession to one's life-style and living standard was determined by heredity. It was this rigid structure, however, that preserved Hindu society through various invasions, including that of the British.


## THE ADVERSARY

British involvement in India began as a capitalistic venture. In the early seventeenth century, the East India Company discovered India to be a bountiful source of spices, jewels, and textiles. The natives were friendly, passive, and fairly easily ruled. The English presence meant the end of the Mogul Empire and Moslem domination. The tiny English minority became the rulers and thus, in effect, the highest of all castes. Anyone who thought to the contrary had to face the British troops that were "protecting" the East India Company.

The British considered India a backward country populated by lethargic, unproductive heathens. That the Indian civilization and culture were far older and in many ways much richer than the British Empire was unimportant to the conquering capitalists. As far as they were concerned, the English presence was a blessing that brought European technology and "civility" to a suffering people.

The Indians had a different opinion, however. As one Hindu philosopher put it, "The day India lost her freedom, a great curse fell on her and she became petrified."

English control stifled the Indian culture and economy. Any Indian who wanted to get ahead had to learn English, attend English schools, and adopt English ways. Conversion to Christianity was a plus. The British, on the other hand, made no attempt to understand or adapt to any part of the age-old Indian way of life. Missionaries tried to convert Indians to Christianity, but never bothered to investigate the very Christian-like qualities of both Hinduism and Islam.

The ultimate purpose of British imperialism was the exploitation of India for the sake of England. The vast area of India was a source of raw materials and agricultural products that could not be produced on the relatively small island of England. In addition, the huge population of India was an enormous market for goods manufactured in England. Consequently, India was gradually milked of its raw materials and its capital.

On August 12, 1858, Queen Victoria became Empress of India when she signed an act making India part of the British Empire. In area, population, and profit, it was the largest component of the Empire, a holding worth fighting to keep. Some 60,000 British troops, led by 10,000 officers and backed by 200,000 native troops, were enough to maintain control. Approximately 2,000 people in the Indian Civil Service administered the country under the leadership of a British viceroy.

To keep the Indians weak, the British created animosity between Hindus and Moslems. A British police chief in Bombay said that by paying Moslems to throw a dead cow into a temple, or Hindus to throw a dead pig into a mosque, he could touch off a riot that would kill hundreds and leave the two religous groups hating each other for years. As long as India remained divided, England could claim that its presence was all that stood between order and anarchy. Hindus and Moslems had been maintaining a peaceful, if not especially friendly, relationship for a thousand years, but three centuries of British meddling had instilled a deep hatred between the two groups.

## THE PROBLEM

This was the India into which Mohandas Gandhi was born. The culture of his country was well over 3,000 years old. Its population of 350 million, second in size only to China's, was divided by religion, language, caste, and geopolitical territories. India was dominated by a foreign power; its economy was supporting a foreign country; its political system was part of a foreign government; and its Eastern culture was being infiltrated and weakened by Western values.

India was in this difficult situation at the beginning of the twentieth century. It was a time when the world, suddenly linked by electronic communication and modern transportation, was becoming as small as a village. Colonialism, or dominance by a foreign power, was dying out. England's economy was slowly sinking. Centers of economic and military power were shifting. Two world wars would be fought before the century was half over.

These were treacherous times for a country in the desperate grip of a foreign power that did not dare let go of its prize possession. The only solution had to be as simple and pure as plain Truth.

# THE BEGINNINGS OF GREATNESS

# 2

"How all this happens—how far a man is free and how far a creature of circumstances— how far free will comes into play and where fate enters on the scene—all this is a mystery and will remain a mystery."

On October 2, 1869, Mohandas Karamchand Gandhi was born, the third son and last of four children in an upper-middle-class family. They were of the Bania subcaste of the Vaisya caste. The Vaisya caste is the third of the four castes into which all Indians are born. The Bania subcaste was traditionally made up of traders and merchants. In fact, "gandhi" means "grocer" in the Gujarati language spoken in the area where Mohandas was born. The word "bania" can also be used as a disparaging term meaning "shrewd, tight-fisted merchant." Ironically, Gandhi the Bania would become a man who ate little and owned nothing to grasp in a tight fist.

Mohandas' father, Karamchand Gandhi, was the sixth generation of Gandhis to serve as prime minister of a princely "state." Such states could be anything from a region of several cities to a single village or even a secluded water well. In charge of each state was a prince who inherited the throne and a hired prime minister to administer the state. For centuries, these states had been independent and often at war with each other.

The Gandhis had served in various states on the Kathiawar peninsula that bulges into the Arabian Sea from northwest India. Karamchand's state was the port city of Porbandar, but his position was more one of prestige than of power. An English governor had authority over the local state; an English viceroy controlled all of India. Karamchand felt little bitterness about this situation, however. He believed that the British had helped India by stopping princely feuds and introducing modern improvements such as railroads and telegraphs.

Mohandas deeply loved and respected his father, but his mother had the strongest influence on him. A devout Hindu and devoted housewife, Putali Ba was always the first to rise and the last to go to bed; all her energy was spent serving her family. That Mohandas would spend his life serving India, mankind, God, and Truth can be attributed, at least in part, to the example set by his mother.

Gandhi's religious convictions and style of worship also followed those of his mother. As a good Hindu, Putali Ba spent part of every day in deep, solitary prayer. She fasted when she felt it was necessary to purify her body and soul as well as to punish herself for shortcomings in her spiritual life. She sometimes vowed not to eat on any day in which she did not see the sun. During the rainy season, this vow meant going without food for several days. Her worried children scanned the skies, calling her outdoors when the sun peeked through the clouds. If she missed seeing the sun, she shrugged and said, "It does not matter. God does not want me to eat today."

Putali Ba belonged to the Vaishnava sect of Hinduism. She believed in both the scriptures of the Hindus and the Koran of the Moslems. Both were correct, she felt, as is any religion that encourages people to look for the difference between right and wrong, to believe that anyone can be better than they are, to contemplate that which is silent and unseen, to pray, and to worship a superior being.

Patuli Ba's ways did not go unnoticed by young Mohandas. Throughout his life he fasted to punish and purify himself and to pressure the consciences of those he wished to change. He also had a strict but broadminded view of religion. Although his life could be seen as one long prayer, the God that he worshipped was not the God of any one religion. To Gandhi, the differences among religions were not important and certainly not something to fight about. He was more interested in that which is common among religions. One of the major goals of his life—and also one of his few failures—was to unite the Hindus and Moslems of his country.

Mohandas married at the age of thirteen—not an early age in Indian tradition but undeniably young in terms of the loving relationship that should exist in a marriage. His wife, Kasturbai, was also thirteen. Since their families had arranged the marriage long before, and since Kasturbai lived in a city far from Porbandar, the young couple did not meet until just before their wedding in 1883.

Though at first she was not much more than a new playmate, Mohandas considered himself lucky to have a wife so pretty and lively. Kasturbai had never learned to read and write, however, and despite her loving husband's efforts, she never mastered these skills. As Mohandas matured and developed profound convictions about life, religion, and politics, Kasturbai could not fully understand him. But she followed him faithfully, trusting him and standing by him as he broke the laws of the British Empire and the centuries-old traditions of India and Hinduism.

MOHANDAS GANDHI:
JUVENILE DELINQUENT

Young Gandhi did not grow up untouched by sin. He learned about it from a friend, a Moslem boy whose identity Mohandas and his family never revealed in later years. Most biographers think he was Sheik Mehtab, the son of the local police chief.

Mehtab spent a great deal of energy and imagination

trying to drag Mohandas into depravity. Although the Gandhi family did not know to what extent Mehtab was influencing their son, they knew he was trouble. When they asked Mohandas why he had such a friend, Mohandas replied, "I am hoping to help him."

Meanwhile, Mehtab was leading his Hindu friend away from the religious path that his ancestors had followed for thousands of years. Mehtab told Mohandas that the British managed to overpower India and control its population (which amounted to one-fifth of the inhabitants on earth), because of their diet. The British ate meat—pork, which was forbidden to Moslems, and beef, the most forbidden of all meats to the vegetarian Hindus. This diet, said Mehtab, gave the British their size, their muscles, and their aggressive ways.

Gandhi had reason to suspect that Mehtab was right. As a proper Hindu, he had never eaten meat; at fifteen, his physical stature was that of a boy five years younger. Mohandas was certainly a lot smaller than Mehtab, who ate meat. Furthermore, his attitudes were hardly aggressive. A shy and passive boy, to avoid a fight he always backed down or arranged a compromise. His mother had taught him that animals, like people, are creatures of God, so neither should kill or eat the other. By not eating meat, she said, one could better meditate on spiritual matters and maintain a pure soul.

Patuli Ba certainly knew much about God, but Mehtab seemed to know more about politics. Young Gandhi, just beginning to develop his life philosophy, felt that politics and religion were separate matters between which one had to choose. If eating meat helped the British to rule India, Mohandas was ready to sacrifice his soul for the freedom of his people.

*Mohandas Gandhi*
*(right) and his brother,*
*Laxmidas, in 1886.*

For the sake of a free India, Mohandas and Mehtab invested in a hunk of goat meat, took it to a secluded river-bank, made a fire, and roasted the "forbidden fruit" on a spit. Mohandas took a bite and gagged. But with the determination that would lead him through far worse, he managed to swallow the meat. Despite the nausea that followed, Mohandas continued to eat meat until he actually began to crave it.

Mehtab's lessons did not end with Mohandas' diet. He next introduced Mohandas to cigarettes. Although they never smoked in public, they practiced in private so that when they were old enough, they would be able to light up like well-practiced adults.

Soon the boys turned to adultery. Mohandas came from a household where his father was not too proud to help with housework and where his wife, although illiterate, had a mind of her own. Thus, Mohandas was a kind and respectful, if somewhat submissive, husband—not a real man, according to Mehtab. What the meek Mohandas needed was an experience with another woman. Their excursion to a brothel on the other side of town did not go well, and the woman Mohandas had hired tossed him out the front door.

With that, young Gandhi's period of delinquency came to an end. Depressed and guilt-ridden, he wrote a detailed letter confessing everything, including a minor theft of family goods and a feeble attempt to commit suicide by eating some supposedly poisonous seeds. In tears, he delivered this confession to his father.

Mohandas never forgot the tears that ran down his father's face. Karamchand, who was extremely ill, thought a moment, tore up the note, and lay back on his cot, knowing that a punishment would not be necessary. Mohandas' "experiments with Truth" came to an end as he signed a vow never to do evil again.


GANDHI GOES TO LONDON

Karamchand's forgiveness instilled in Mohandas a profound love. As his father's health deteriorated, his youngest son was at his side as much as possible, trying to nurse him back to health but succeeding only in making him more comfortable as he approached death. Karamchand finally died during the few moments when Mohandas went to lie with his wife, giving the young man a life-long sense of guilt.

Mohandas passed his college entrance examinations and went to study at a small school on the west coast of India. Though his grades reflected a lack of enthusiasm, his older brother wisely suggested that Mohandas go to law school in London. With such an education he would be better equipped to carry on the honor, wealth, and good name of the Gandhi family, and perhaps even become their seventh prime minister.

The eighteen-year-old boy who boarded the steamship out of Bombay in September 1888 was no man of the world. He had never read an English newspaper and had had little contact with British citizens. In fact, he had never even seen a large city until he traveled to Bombay to ask the elders of the Bania subcaste for permission to cross the ocean, an act prohibited in the Hindu religion.

Such permission did not come easily from either the elders or his family. Both knew that life outside India was based on different values, and that worldly temptations often proved irresistible. The caste elders forbade the trip, so Gandhi's departure caused him to be thrown out of the Bania subcaste, a stigma that left him without friends or social contacts, almost an Untouchable. But Mohandas Gandhi took on that title with pride.

His mother agreed to let him go only after he took three solemn vows: never to eat meat, never to drink alcohol, and never to forget his marriage vows of fidelity to his wife. During his three years in London, he successfully resisted these temptations, while breaking other traditional rules upheld by the elders. Thus, at the age of eighteen he began to learn to follow only those laws, traditions, and rules that he felt in his heart were right.

The temptations of the Western world began with the fifty-day voyage from Bombay to London. Given a menu in the dining room, Mohandas saw an impressive list of meat dishes but not much else. At that first meal he contented himself with bread, butter, and tea. He imagined himself trying to use a knife and fork as the English diners did. Like most Indians, he ate by picking up his food with clean fingers. Uncomfortable at the thought of using utensils, he swore never to return to the dining room, choosing to live off the few fruits and sweets he had in his trunk.

Hoping to make a good impression upon his arrival in London, he dressed as he had always seen the British in the hot streets of India, in spotless white cotton. But when the ship docked on a cool, cloudy day in late October, everyone except Mohandas Gandhi was wearing dark, heavy clothes.

The incident was more than embarrassing. Young Gandhi began to realize that clothes function almost as a uniform, a message telling something about the person wearing them. The message he wore as he walked down the gangplank said, "This man is not from around here."

Immediately, Mohandas bought a dapper version of the local uniform. He wanted to fit in, to be "more English than an Englishman." Later, as he learned to be himself and to let his actions speak rather than his uniform, he would reject stylish clothing. He often wore no more than the *dhoti* loincloth he would one day sport in the presence of the King of England.

As a young man in London, however, his concerns were split between trying to be British and trying to get into and through London University Law School. Mohandas bought fashionable clothes and took French, dancing, and violin lessons. He was an utter failure at all but dressing, and even that too quickly consumed his meager budget. After failing the London University entrance examination because he didn't know Latin, he began to study in earnest.

He had found a boarding room where the landlady, to keep her tenant from starving, agreed to prepare special vegetarian meals. His stomach rejoiced when he finally found a vegetarian restaurant, and his soul rejoiced at meeting the people who ate there. Since they were vegetarians due to philosophical reasons, Mohandas had much to discuss with them. They formed a vegetarian society. A scholar among them, Sir Edwin Arnold, was an authority on the *Bhagavad Gita*. This epic poem of Indian history and Hindu morality, though not considered the word of God, was a veritable book of scriptures and prayers for Hindus. Yet until then, Mohandas had never read it.

Here began another stage in Gandhi's extracurricular education. He passionately studied not only the *Gita* but also the works of other religions. The Old Testament tales of fear and punishment he did not like, but the New Testament philosophy of loving thy neighbor, forgiving enemies, and turning the other cheek "went straight to my heart," he said, "like the *Gita*!" Later in life he would study the Moslem Koran and the writings of the Buddha, all of which contained parts of the great Truth that was Gandhi's God.

## OFF TO AFRICA

After a year at London University, Gandhi passed his final examinations. On June 10, 1891 he was "called to the bar" to receive a license to practice law as an English barrister. Two days later he was bound for Bombay, only to disembark and receive the news that his mother had died a few days after his graduation.

He survived the ensuing grief with the help of his wife and the baby boy who had been born a few months after Mohandas had left for London. To support them, he took the only job he could find, which was little more than a legal secretary to some prominent barristers. It didn't take him long to tire of preparing legal briefs and drawing up simple petitions for peasants who were hoping for help from the local government. It also didn't take him long to see that his colleagues in the legal field were more interested in impressing and winning the favors of Indian princes and British officials than in law and justice.

An opportunity to escape from this rut came in early 1893. The Dada Abdullah Company, a group of Moslem merchants in South Africa, needed someone with a knowledge of the English language and the British legal system. Although Mohandas suspected he was stepping out of one rut and into another, he kissed Kasturbai and his son good-bye and booked a first-class cabin on a boat bound for the port of Durban in the state of Natal in the British colony of South Africa.

# RACISM RULES

## 3

"It has always been a mystery to me how men can feel themselves honored by the humiliation of their fellow-beings."

It did not take Gandhi long to learn about life in South Africa. Dada Abdullah, not sure what sort of man he had hired, took Gandhi to a trial in Durban. They both wanted to test the compatibility of the London-educated Indian barrister and the South African legal system.

If clothes are a uniform that tell something about the wearer, what Gandhi wore into the courtroom marked a man torn between two cultures as he entered a third. His clothes were those of an English barrister, an image he very much wanted to project. But on his head he wore the traditional turban of India, a country he could neither forsake nor forget. He was neither the only man wearing a turban nor the only man wearing English clothes. But he was the only one wearing both.

The judge asked the Indian to remove his headgear. Gandhi refused, the judge insisted, and the new barrister walked out of the courtroom.

Back at the office, Dada Abdullah explained not only court rules but also South African social rules. In court, anyone who was English or anyone dressed in western clothes had to remove their hat. The law recognized, however, that Arab Moslems considered wearing a turban a religious right. Therefore, they did not have to remove them in court. For the sake of convenience, Indian Moslems such as Dada Abdullah wore Moslem garb and so would pass as Arabs. But non-Moslem Indians wore no such clothes and thus had no such right.

Hoping to preserve his image and solve the problem, Gandhi wanted to compromise by wearing an English hat that he would be required to remove but that would not be a symbolical shedding of his religion. But Dada Abdullah said that only Christian Indians wore English clothes and hats, and they were usually waiters, clerks, and others low on the socio-economic scale. Furthermore, Gandhi's compromise would be an insult to all Indians.

Abdullah's solution was not to go back to the courtroom. Gandhi's response was a letter of protest to the editor of a local newspaper. This act of courage and defiance impressed the Moslem merchant. By the time the letter was published, however, Gandhi was on a train to Pretoria, in the Dutch-controlled Transvaal area of South Africa, where Abdullah kept his main office.

South Africa had been settled by the Dutch in the seventeenth century. When the British seized the southern portion in 1806, the Dutch (called Boers) moved north. There they founded the colonial territories of the Transvaal and the Free Orange State. The British maintained control over the southern territories of Natal and the Cape Colony.

As Gandhi would soon discover, the court incident in Durban was an indication of the deep and pervasive racism throughout Africa. European whites were considered supreme in all matters. Other citizens, including Indians, Chinese, and local black natives, were known as "coloreds" and were often addressed by such lowly names as "coolie" and "Sammi."

The so-called coloreds had virtually no political or social rights. Indians who came to South Africa as indentured laborers, although considered slightly superior to local blacks, were not much better off than slaves. They came to South Africa under an agreement that they would work for five years at very low wages and then receive either passage back to India or freedom to stay as second-class citizens. Freed or indentured, only those Indians living in British territory had the right to vote. Indians sharing hotels, restaurants, or train compartments with whites were subjected to indefinite rules. How strictly they were enforced depended on such factors as the dress and apparent cleanliness of the Indian and the prejudice of the whites involved. But it was always the whites who decided.

Despite his well-groomed appearance, Gandhi had trouble on the train to the Transvaal. Abdullah had bought him a first-class ticket for a sleeping berth, but a white man announced that he would not sleep in the presence of a "coolie." A conductor was fetched and Gandhi was told to move to the third-class coach. He refused, the conductor insisted, and ten minutes later the Indian was sitting on a station platform, his baggage in the custody of the stationmaster, and his train chugging away into the distance.

The night was cold. With no overcoat and no place to sleep, Gandhi could only shiver and think. As he later wrote in his autobiography, he came to some important conclusions. "The hardship to which I was subjected was superficial—only a symptom of the deep disease of color prejudice. I should try, if possible, to root out the disease and suffer hardship in the process." He realized that he was prepared, because of his past experiences, to work toward reforming an intolerable situation. Few Indians in South Africa had a knowledge of the law and the deep religious convictions that considered prejudice and injustice a contradiction to the Truth that was, to Gandhi, God.

The next morning, Gandhi sent a letter of protest to the

general manager of the railroad. He then took the next train to the end of the line. From there he took a stagecoach north to Johannesburg where he could connect with the Transvaal train system of the Boer territory. As he boarded the stage-coach with a first-class ticket, he again became the victim of prejudice. The conductor would not allow a colored to ride among the whites. Rather than delay his trip further, Gandhi agreed to ride up front with the driver. The conductor sat inside in the seat Gandhi had paid for. Later, however, the conductor wanted to smoke his pipe and so requested Gandhi's seat outside beside the driver. This meant Gandhi had to move to an even more degrading position—the footstep of the coach. This time he refused. As the conductor began to beat him and pull him away, the other passengers protested, saying that they didn't mind if he rode with them. Gandhi finally got the seat he had paid for.

In Johannesburg, after sending a letter of protest to the stage company, Gandhi tried to check into the Grand National Hotel. He was told what any South African Indian would have been told: "Sorry, sir. No vacancies." Fortunately, Gandhi had the address of an Indian in town and found a place to sleep there.

The next day on the train to Pretoria, where Gandhi was sitting peacefully in a compartment with an Englishman, the conductor ordered him back to the third-class coach. Gandhi refused, and fortunately the Englishman told the conductor what he thought of such prejudice. The passenger insisted that Gandhi stay with him.

The incident impressed Gandhi. This was the kind of behavior he had learned to expect from the British—just, civil, and humane. Twenty years later, when he was negotiating with the British in India; he would continue to assume that their words and their intentions were as good as those of the English people he had met earlier in his life.

In Pretoria, again wondering where he would sleep, Gandhi chanced to meet an American as kind as the Englishman, a black American who knew well the problem of finding a vacancy in a decent hotel. He had an American friend who owned a hotel and he invited Gandhi to stay there. After asking the permission of his other guests, the proprietor not only invited Gandhi to eat in the dining room but served him a vegetarian meal as well.

"IS THIS CIVILIZATION?"

The next day Gandhi found permanent lodging with a poor couple who were willing to overlook his skin color and strange diet if it meant extra income. Gandhi, however, was not willing to forget all that had happened on his journey from Durban. When it turned out that Dada Abdullah's office had little work for him, he began devoting his talents and energies to fighting racism.

A few days after his arrival, he called a meeting of all Indians living in Pretoria. There he learned the depth of their plight. They could not own land except in certain areas; they could not vote; they had to pay an annual tax simply because they were Indian; they could not use the sidewalks; they had to stay off the streets after 9:00 P.M.; and at no time could they walk down the street where the Boer president lived.

At the age of twenty-three, Mohandas Gandhi stood boldly before his compatriots in Pretoria. Unlike many rising leaders in other times and places, he did not call for the overthrow of the oppressors or even for an immediate confrontation. First, he said, Indians would have to make themselves worthy of equality. For example, the Boers forced the Indians to live in separate areas, supposedly for reasons of sanitation. The Indians should respond, said Gandhi, with fastidious cleanliness. They were not allowed to vote because they were uneducated. Many Indians did not understand English, the predominant language in both British and Boer territories. The Indians should educate themselves, said Gandhi. And so they could not be accused of dishonesty, they should adopt a policy of scrupulous ethics, especially in business. They were considered unworthy of democracy because they bickered among themselves and remained divided over the differences between the Moslem and Hindu religions. To solve this most important problem, Gandhi told them that they must unite as brothers, regardless of religion.

His pleas were heeded. Hindus and Moslems worked together, for the first time in years, to clean up their neighborhoods. They taught each other English. Three months later, Gandhi wrote a letter to a newspaper in Durban. He pointed out that Indians led simple lives, worked hard, saved their money, and abstained from alcohol. Accusations of ignorance, dishonesty, and unsanitary practices were unfounded. Suggesting that these accusations might be the cause of the hatred against these good British subjects, Gandhi asked: "Is this Christian-like, is this fair play, is this justice, is this civilization?"


## A NEW SOLUTION

For the next year, Gandhi worked hard to help Indians improve themselves and their public image. He also solved Dada Abdullah's lawsuit, the reason he had been called to South Africa in the first place.

The suit had been in the courts for a long time, with lawyers on both sides using legal technicalities to make the case drag on as long as possible. Gandhi saw that the lawyers were getting richer while Abdullah and the opposing party, who was also a Moslem Indian, were getting poorer.

"Lawyers are leeches living off the blood of their clients," he later wrote in his autobiography. Abdullah and his adversary apparently shared this opinion. Gandhi was able to convince them to solve their differences without courts or lawyers. They agreed on an arbitrator, explained their positions clearly and quickly, and accepted the arbitrator's decision, which awarded Abdullah £37,000.

Gandhi's idea of justice did not end there. The merchant who lost the case would go bankrupt if he had to pay the full amount at once. For a Moslem, bankruptcy is a disgrace that drives some to suicide. Gandhi explained this to Abdullah, and though not required by law or custom to cooperate, the two merchants agreed to an installment plan for gradual payment of the money.

This was justice to Mohandas Gandhi—not something determined in courts or defined by law but rather a compromise in which two parties benefited. His unprecedented success in this case showed him that his job as a lawyer would not be to fight for or against any one side. To establish justice, he would find out the facts and then mediate between opposing parties to guide them toward a solution that neither could deny. For the next fifty years, he would carry this principle from the slums of Bombay to the halls of British Parliament.

A year later, having met if not directly worked with virtually every Indian in Pretoria, Gandhi prepared to return to India and his wife and two sons. But at a good-bye party in Durban he happened to see a newspaper article about the Indian Franchise Bill. The bill, if passed, would deprive Indians in the British colony of the right to vote for the National Assembly.

"This is the first nail in our coffin," he declared to a friend at the party. Although the Indians present had neither known nor cared about the bill, at Gandhi's call to arms, the party turned into a working committee.

The committee wrote a petition, made five copies, and took them door to door around Durban. Another copy went to the newspapers. They sent telegrams to the prime minister asking that the legislation be postponed. He deferred it for two days—not enough time for the Indians to prepare a proper defense of their interests.

The all-white National Assembly passed the bill, but Gandhi hoped to prevent its final approval by the Colonial Secretary in London. A petition with ten thousand signatures

— 29 —

convinced the secretary to veto the bill, but the National Assembly soon passed a similar bill that achieved the same end without directly mentioning Indians. Gandhi considered it a victory of principle in a battle by no means over.

Some time previously, the Indians in India had established the Indian National Congress. Though it had no governing power, through the Congress Indians could make their feelings known to their British overlords. Gandhi, realizing Indians in South Africa needed a more powerful organization, established the Natal National Congress in August 1894. As its secretary, he made the Natal National Congress a much more effective vehicle than the Indian National Congress.

In a campaign similar to the one Gandhi had started in Pretoria, the Natal National Congress promoted education, sanitation, and unification. It took on an additional cause when an indentured laborer stumbled into Gandhi's house with torn clothes and a bleeding mouth. The man had been beaten by the owner of the plantation where he worked. The police would do nothing to help him, and the man was required by law to return to work. Gandhi was his only hope.

Gandhi took the case to court, and even agreed to remove his turban there. Seeking the release of the laborer rather than revenge against the cruel employer, he won the case. It was the first time an indentured laborer had fought for his or her rights in South Africa.

At that time, indentured laborers who completed their term of work had to choose between returning to India, beginning a new indentured contract, or buying freedom at £25 per family per year, which, for most foreign workers, was almost a year's pay. After numerous petitions from the Natal National Congress and newspaper editorials written by Mohandas Gandhi, the British Viceroy of India registered an objection to the way his subjects were being treated in South Africa. The tax on purchasing freedom was then lowered to £3 per year per person. For large Indian families, this situation was not much better than before. But it showed that Gandhi and the Natal Congress were being heard in London and India as well as in South Africa.

In 1896, Gandhi returned to India to pick up Kasturbai and their sons. He spent six months there trying to improve the South African situation by distributing pamphlets, publishing letters, and conferring with British officials. Then he and his family boarded a boat filled with four hundred indentured workers bound for South Africa. That boat was joined by another. The two boats presented quite a problem in Durban.

Because of an outbreak of the bubonic plague in Bombay, all incoming boats had to spend a quarantine period of five days at anchor in Durban harbor. But the presence of Gandhi and some eight hundred Indians worried British officials. The white population of Durban had heard of Gandhi's activism, though few of them really knew what he had been preaching. As the quarantine was extended to sixteen days and then twenty-three days, ugly rumors spread among the whites. When Gandhi was finally allowed to land, a rowdy crowd awaited him on the dock.

Gandhi sent his family ashore in disguise and under protection. But Gandhi knew that sooner or later he would have to walk the streets. Now was a good time to start. Accompanied only by an English friend, he proceeded through the crowd. Rocks, bottles, garbage, and jeers rained down on them.

Suddenly Gandhi was separated from his friend. A group of teenagers caught hold of his turban and pulled it off. Then they began kicking and punching him. As he clung to a railing, losing consciousness, blood poured from a cut on his neck. Fortunately, the wife of the Durban police chief happened to come along. She courageously entered the fray to help Gandhi. As she shielded him with her open parasol, the attackers, afraid to harm a woman—especially the police chief's wife—backed off. With the help of two constables, Gandhi and the woman made their way to the house of an Indian merchant. The crowd followed, surrounded the house, and chanted "Let's hang Gandhi from the sour apple tree . . ." until they learned that their prey had escaped over a back fence and down an alley.

GANDHI: WAR HERO

Kasturbai was shocked to see the life that her husband, a successful lawyer, was leading in Durban. Although he had enough money to buy a house, he cut his own hair and did his own laundry by hand in order to dedicate more funds to helping the poor and oppressed. Furthermore, his home was a commune inhabited by several aides and friends, including some Untouchables. Mohandas and Kasturbai had quite a spat when he asked her to empty the chamber pot of an Untouchable and smile cheerfully while doing so. She managed to perform only the first part of the request.

There was constant activity. The Natal Congress grew in strength, but the campaign to improve the public image of the Indian population had little effect. The government passed two new bills, one requiring Indian merchants to buy licenses, and another requiring immigrants to pass an English test in order to enter or to stay in the British colony.

In 1899 the Boer War broke out. The Boers of the Transvaal wanted to free their gold mines of British ownership and, if possible, force the British out of Natal. As the Boer army pushed into Natal, it looked as if they might succeed.

In a move that impressed everyone, Gandhi chose to support the British rather than stay out of the fight. Since he was a British subject, he felt obliged to defend British interests. He also hoped, once again, that the British, known to be fair-minded, would reward South African Indians for their loyalty. He and his compatriots did not take up arms, but they formed the Indian Ambulance Corps.

At first the Natal government refused the services of

these "coolie volunteers." But as British casualties mounted, Gandhi and his corps of eleven hundred Indians—most of them indentured workers—risked their lives on the battlefront to save British soldiers. After the war ended and England had established control over the Transvaal, Gandhi and his volunteers received several medals for facing direct gunfire in order to help others.

With newspapers and the public in England and South Africa now praising the patriotism and capabilities of Indians, Gandhi felt his work in Natal was complete. In 1901 he returned to India, leaving behind thousands of dollars worth of jewels he had received as gifts. The jewels were put in a trust fund to support the causes Gandhi had initiated in South Africa.

Gandhi received a hero's welcome in India. Indians had heard of his good works in South Africa and they wanted him to do the same in India. The Indian National Congress was already in progress in Calcutta, so he headed there first.

He was appalled at what he found. The Congress was meeting in a large tent on the outskirts of town. The throngs that attended were in complete disarray. The caste system was operating in full force. Pompous Brahmin leaders were more concerned about their own power than the causes of the Congress. Arguments ensued about who should clean the latrines or deliver messages.

Gandhi recognized this as a form of racism. To demonstrate its absurdity, he himself, the most respected man present, grabbed a mop and bucket and began cleaning latrines.

His willingness to do the work of the Untouchable achieved little more than the temporary embarrassment of the men who were trying to uphold their false importance. Gandhi did manage, however, to get the Congress to pass a resolution supporting his work in South Africa. Although accepted unanimously, it was little more than words without any power to back them.

The Congress closed and Gandhi set up a law business in Bombay. Not long after, however, the Natal National Congress summoned him back to South Africa to deal with an emergency.

## PHOENIX FARM

The progress that Gandhi and the South African Indians had made was eroding quickly. As a result of the Boer War, the British and Boer territories were to be joined as the Union of South Africa. The Indians in the Transvaal were not enjoying the respect that those of Natal had earned through their heroic participation in the Boer War. The Birtish rulers, who would now control the entire area, preferred to keep peace with the Boers rather than with the indentured workers and freed Indians of the Transvaal.

Gandhi knew his work would be in the Transvaal, so he opened a law office in Johannesburg. There he defended poor Indians in court. He also started a weekly newspaper, *Indian Opinion,* which was printed in Durban and distributed all over South Africa.

*Indian Opinion* had three purposes: to guide Indians toward self-improvement, to give the Indian community an identity and a voice, and to publicly defend Indians against the misinformation that was rampant in the white community. Although advertising space and some three thousand subscriptions were sold, profit was not the purpose of *Indian Opinion.* In fact, it began to lose money and approach bankruptcy.

Knowing that *Indian Opinion* was of utmost importance to the defense of South African Indians, Gandhi boarded a train

*Mohandas and Kasturbai*
*after their return to*
*India from South Africa.*

for the twenty-four-hour trip to the printing office in Durban. During that trip he read a book, John Ruskin's *Unto This Last,* that would reveal to him a new level of philosophical awareness. As he wrote in a later issue of *Indian Opinion,* the book helped him formulate three major ideas:

1: The good of the individual is contained in the good of all; that is, the more one gives to society, the more one gains personally. (This he had already known but had never seen expressed elsewhere.)

2. A lawyer's work has the same value as a barber's; that is, both have the right to earn a living, but neither is more valuable than the other. (This, too, Gandhi had long suspected.)

3. The life of manual labor is the life truly worth living. (This was something new to Gandhi.)

He resolved to act on these ideas immediately. The next day, he entered the *Indian Opinion* printshop and announced a drastic change to his employees. The shop was to be moved out of the city to a farm, where all employees would earn the same pay and would be expected to live together in a self-sufficient commune.

A few could not accept these conditions, but most shared Gandhi's excitement and idealism. Fourteen miles (22 km) from Durban, near the town of Phoenix, they found a one-hundred-acre plot with a spring, some fruit trees, and a lot of snakes. Gandhi told his employees if they ignored the snakes, the snakes would ignore them—an absurd idea that actually worked. With the help of the old Ambulance Corps, they put up crude housing and connected the printing press to a hand-cranked wheel. Miraculously, the scheme worked. *Indian Opinion* survived and the life-style of the people who wrote and printed it would serve as a model for future communes.

## ZULUS AND A NEW GANDHI

Gandhi divided himself between Johannesburg and Phoenix Farm, as it became known, until 1906. Early in that year, a Zulu chieftain speared a British tax collector, touching off a rebellion in Zululand. The British counterattacked. Gandhi, still a loyal British subject, offered the services of the Ambulance Corps.

Gandhi and his crew soon discovered the true nature of the British counterinsurgency campaign. It was not bringing peace to Zululand but, instead, teaching its inhabitants a lesson with such cruel tactics as public hangings and floggings. The Indian Ambulance Corps ended up treating wounded Zulus rather than British soldiers.

In *Indian Opinion* Gandhi wrote:

> We had to clean the wounds of several Zulus which
> had not been attended to for as many as five or six
> days and were therefore stinking horribly. We liked
> our work. The Zulus could not talk to us, but from
> their gestures and the expression in their eyes, they
> seemed to feel as if God had sent us to their suc-
> cor.

Gandhi's experiences with the Zulus inspired a radical change in his life. At the age of thirty-six, to serve humanity with all the powers of his soul, he adopted three principles that would govern his every action for the rest of his life. He would be celibate, never again having sexual relations with his wife or any other woman. He would practice *ahimsa,* a policy of non-violence toward all living creatures. And he would fight injustice and violence with *satyagraha,* the force of Truth and love.

# GANDHI'S TRUTH

## 4

*". . . those who say that religion has nothing to do with politics do not know what religion means."*

The first three chapters of this book have referred to a special Truth. During this first half of his life Gandhi was gradually realizing the nature and importance of a pure Truth. As he came to understand this Truth, his life changed radically. At this point, we would do well to try to understand Gandhi's Truth.

Gandhi said that Truth is whatever one feels in one's heart is morally good, correct, and true. Truth is revealed by a silent inner voice. Everyone feels a different and contrary Truth because human minds evolve in different ways. Truth for one person is different from Truth for another. No one can fully understand Truth because it is infinite and people are imperfect. Therefore, no one should try to force one's own version of the Truth on another person. Not only does no one possess the ultimate Truth, but the violence of force is a contradiction of Truth. No force can create or alter Truth.

The ultimate Truth was Gandhi's God. He said that all religions were attempts to describe this Truth, or this God. He regarded Jesus as a supreme artist because in the Sermon on the Mount he expressed Truth so eloquently. Mohammed, too, saw the Truth and described it in the Koran, the most beautiful of all Arabic writings. The Buddha also knew the Truth and had yet another way of describing it. None of these religions is right or wrong, according to Gandhi. There are a million ways to describe God. The descriptions of God and goodness that all religions share are parts of the Truth that is God.

It is interesting that although Gandhi thoroughly accepted the Christian morality, he did not believe that Jesus was God's only son. He believed that all creatures, humans and animals alike, are the children of God. Jesus was superior only insofar as he understood the Truth. In a similar way, humans are superior to animals in that people are capable of seeking the Truth and of making moral decisions about what they do. Animals have no such free will and thus are locked into a world of violence. Humans are capable of rising above violence by understanding the Truth.

## TRUTH *VERSUS* VIOLENCE

*Ahimsa* is the Hindu word for nonviolence. But meaning much more, it encompasses the ideas of truth, love, justice, brotherhood, harmony, and goodwill. Gandhi called *ahimsa* the greatest force available to humanity. *Ahimsa* is upheld by the power of the Truth, while violence is in direct contradiction and conflict with Truth. In such a confrontation, Truth always wins in the long run.

*Ahimsa* is the opposite of *himsa*. Animals and people are born with *himsa*; it does not have to be taught. It is a natural and instinctive preoccupation with the physical well-being and comfort of the body. *Himsa* does not hesitate to use violence to gain what the physical body desires. Violence, in this sense, includes force, aggression, hatred, lying, and cheating. *Ahimsa*, on the other hand, is a spiritual characteristic. It is above the desires of the body and it is nonviolent. It must be learned, and only humans have the free will to choose to seek and learn it. It is not an easy state to attain, but it is all that distinguishes humans from animals.

Gandhi made his vow of celibacy in order to achieve greater control over his physical desires. By subduing *himsa* and enriching *ahimsa*, he hoped to come closer to God and an understanding of the Truth. His practice of fasting had the similar purpose of starving the body to feed the soul.

Gandhi was called Christ-like for his ability to withstand any pain and hardship, to deny himself physical comforts, and to live unencumbered by material possessions. He was always ready to die if it meant the preservation of the goodness and pureness of the *ahimsa* in his soul. In fact, he felt that the death of the physical body would rid him of the *himsa* he had. At death, he would truly understand Truth and God.

SATYAGRAHA

Gandhi sensed a mysterious Power pervading everything in the universe. This Power is part of the Truth. It sustains the Truth just as the Truth generates the Power. This Power is above and beyond perception by the human senses. It cannot be proven by logic or studied by science. But it is there and it is with those who are living and acting in accordance with the Truth.

Gandhi felt that this Power gave strength to his *satyagraha* campaigns. *Satyagraha* literally means truth and firmness, or Truth-force. As Gandhi used it, it was the means by which *ahimsa* was carried into politics and social reform. This more popular meaning is often defined as "passive resistance." It is a way of fighting without hating or hurting. By disobeying unjust laws, refusing to cooperate with authorities, and boycotting certain goods or industries, an oppressed people can resist their oppressors without physically attacking them.

Through *satyagraha*, as we shall see in succeeding chapters, Gandhi used the nonviolent and spiritual power of the Truth to confront and overcome the violent physical power of the British Empire.

All of Gandhi's political activities were outgrowths of his religious beliefs. Religion and politics were not separate; he felt that while government, politics, and law are necessary in this world, one must obey one's religious convictions first. One must resist the rules of a government that contradict the morals of one's religion or the demands of one's conscience. *Satyagraha* was Gandhi's connecting link between religion and politics. Its principles and policies were those of his religious morality, and its objectives were changes in India's political system.

## CHILDREN OF GOD

When young Mohandas disobeyed the elders of the Bania subcaste by going to London, he was excommunicated from his caste. It did not matter that he had kept his vows to obey the Hindu rules. But because he was thrown out of his caste, he was, technically, an Untouchable. Until the elders of another subcaste agreed to forgive him for his "sin," he could not enter the house or share the meal of even his closest relatives.

Gandhi was not against India's caste system. He felt that it was part of the fabric that held Indian society together. But he saw the abuses which took place within the system. To Gandhi it did not matter if one was born into a certain caste. The immorality was the assumption that people in different castes were not equal, that Brahmins were superior to Sudras, that Untouchables were no more important than vermin. This, he said, was contrary to the Truth of *ahimsa*.

While millions of Indians thought that contact with even the shadow of an Untouchable meant self-pollution, Gandhi would not hesitate to clean their chamber pots or share food from his plate with them. He replaced the term Untouchable with *harijan*, or "Children of God." He called the concept of untouchability "a device of Satan and the greatest of all blots on Hinduism." He said repeatedly that Indian "self-government is inconceivable and unattainable without the removal of untouchability;" otherwise Indians would treat their own people just as the British had treated Indians.

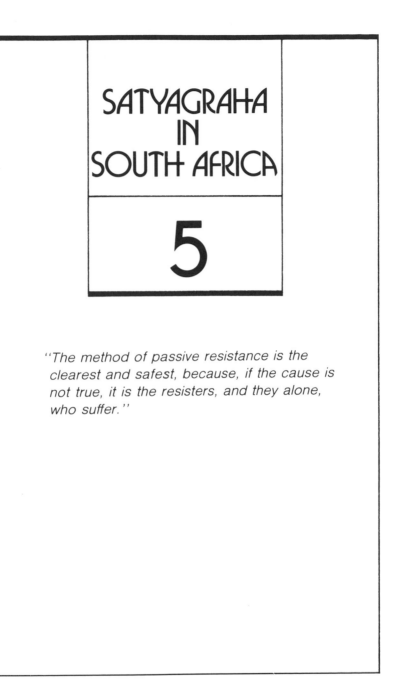

# SATYAGRAHA IN SOUTH AFRICA

# 5

*"The method of passive resistance is the clearest and safest, because, if the cause is not true, it is the resisters, and they alone, who suffer."*

In September 1906, the government of the Transvaal was on the verge of passing the Asiatic Law Amendment Ordinance. It would require all Indians to register with the government, submit a complete set of fingerprints, and carry a registration certificate at all times. Police could demand to see this certificate without any reason and even enter private homes without permission to check registrations.

The Indians saw this as the beginning of slavery. Like dogs, they would be required to carry licenses. Like criminals, they would be identified by fingerprints. Like prisoners on parole, they could not go far from home.

Gandhi called a mass protest meeting at a theater in Johannesburg, and some three thousand Indians showed up. With the help of translators, Gandhi explained the Ordinance so that Indians of all dialects could understand. He then proposed a resolution that all Indians refuse to obey the Ordinance if it became law. Speaker after speaker gave their opinions on the resolution, which they dubbed "The Black Act," until one man said that he would do more than just vote with the majority. He would make a public vow with God that, regardless of the passage or failure of the resolution, he, as an individual, would not obey the Black Act.

To Gandhi, a vow invoking God was a very serious matter. He approved, but warned the crowd that a vow cannot be taken lightly. Adhering to such a vow would mean imprisonment, hunger, fines, and quite likely beatings by police or jailers. If a vow was made bravely one day but forgotten the next, it would be worthless. But if just a few Indians managed to keep their vows, he told them, their righteousness would prove more powerful than the government.

To Gandhi's surprise, the entire audience stood up, raised their right hands, and vowed to God that they would resist the Black Act.

The idea of resisting the unjust law, which was soon passed by the National Assembly, spread throughout South Africa. To give the movement a name, Gandhi coined the word *satyagraha*—the force of Truth. Those who practiced it were called *satyagrahis*.

The Indians stuck to their vows. Only a few hundred out of the thirteen thousand in the Transvaal registered. Gandhi and other leaders were given two-month jail sentences which they accepted without resistance. As increasing numbers of *satyagrahis* were arrested, the jails began to fill up. The Minister of Indian Affairs, General Jan Christiaan Smuts, proposed a compromise to Gandhi. The registration ordinance would be repealed and the resisters would be released from jail if they agreed to register voluntarily.

To everyone's amazement, Gandhi consented. He resolved to be the first to register. But as he approached the registration office, he was attacked from behind and knocked unconscious by an Indian of the Pathan tribe. When Gandhi awakened in the house of a friend, the first thing he did was forgive the Pathan; then he signed the registration papers.

Trusting Gandhi's judgment, many Indians followed his example. But when General Smuts later failed to repeal the ordinance as promised, Gandhi launched another *satyagraha*.

He and most other Indians publicly burned their registration cards and soon found themselves back in jail.

Gandhi discovered jail to be a perfect place to fast, pray, think, and read. There he first read Henry David Thoreau's *Civil Disobedience*. There, Gandhi's beliefs were confirmed: it is better to please your soul than your government; every person has the right and obligation to resist an unjust law; and a single determined person can effect a change in even the most powerful government.

## TOLSTOY FARM

When the *satyagrahis* were arrested, they often lost what little they owned. Upon their release, they and their families were destitute. To help them survive in both body and spirit, Gandhi founded a communal farm modeled after the Phoenix Farm.

He named it Tolstoy Farm after the Russian author who in later life became profoundly religious and wrote one of the books that most influenced Gandhi: *The Kingdom of God Is Within You*. Like the people who would live on the eleven-hundred-acre farm outside of Johannesburg, Count Leo Tolstoy had given up his possessions, disdained money, avoided tobacco and alcohol, refused to kill animals or eat meat, wore simple clothes, and spent the rest of his life doing manual labor and preaching that one's highest duty on earth was to love others, resist tyranny, and refrain from violence.

The men, women, and children of Tolstoy Farm lived as a single family. To prepare themselves for their passive battle against tyranny, they met with Gandhi every day to discuss the virtues of *ahimsa*, *satyagraha*, self-denial, self-sacrifice, and self-reliance. Together they said prayers from the *Bhagavad Gita* and sang hymns from various religions. They grew their own food and made their own houses, furniture, and clothes.

During this time, Gandhi began regular seven-day fasting periods. When he ate, he restricted his diet to fruit, nuts, raw cereal, and olive oil. Self-denial made him feel stronger, and he suspected that it purified not only his own soul but those around him as well. He also declared that, for him, Monday would be a day of silence. For the rest of his life he would never utter a word on a Monday.

## THE ARMY OF PEACE

The Black Act continued in effect but was left unenforced and largely ignored during the time Gandhi developed Tolstoy Farm and the British and Boers created the Union of South Africa. Under the agreement that had ended the Boer War, Boer and British territories were to be united as a single member of the British Commonwealth. The transition called for a new government. The Boers became British subjects. It was a politically and socially awkward change.

There was little conflict between Indians and the government until 1913, when a Supreme Court decision refused to recognize as legal any marriages that had not been registered with the government. The Hindus and Moslems, who considered marriage a pact between husband, wife, and God, were outraged. Because of this court decision, almost all Indian wives legally became mere concubines and their children illegitimate.

The intolerable situation raised up another *satyagraha* throughout the Union of South Africa. Just as the three-pound head-tax on freed indentured workers had brought the poor into politics, the mass marriage annulment involved women and children. As was his policy, Gandhi first warned the government to repeal both laws or face another *satyagraha*. South African Prime Minister General Louis Botha did not even bother to respond.

The first to sacrifice themselves were sixteen women, among them Kasturbai, from Phoenix Farm. They crossed into the Transvaal from Natal without government permission and were promptly arrested. A few days later, eleven women from Tolstoy Farm marched into Natal and then on to the coal

*Gandhi kept a day of silence every Monday. Here, on his day of silence, he lies blindfolded as his message to an East Bengal village is read aloud.*

mines of New Castle. There they exhorted the indentured mine workers to strike in protest of the unjust laws and the cruel arrest of the women from Phoenix Farm.

The laborers dropped their tools and returned to the company-owned buildings where they lived. It was the first strike by nonwhites in South Africa and it had the company owners worried. To frighten the strikers, they shut off the water and electricity to the housing compound and beat up a few workers. Gandhi, who had rushed to the scene, called for all Indians to leave the compound and set up camp at a near-by plot of land. They did so, taking with them only their clothes and blankets. After frantic efforts to find and prepare food for them, Gandhi decided to march them north to the Transvaal and, quite likely, prison. He explained the principles of *satyagraha* to them, warned them of the dangers, and asked the unsure to stay behind.

They all followed. With some six thousand men, women, and children in tow, Gandhi crossed into the Transvaal. There he demanded either the repeal of the Black Act and the court marriage decision, or the arrest of his entire "army of peace." The government refused to do either. Gandhi's army, denied room and board in "His Majesty's hotel," marched north toward Tolstoy Farm.

Gandhi was arrested twice along the way but was quickly released because no one else could control the swollen ranks of his ragtag army. Finally, just short of Tolstoy Farm, Gandhi was arrested, charged with illegally crossing the border, and given a nine-month jail sentence. The *satyagrahis* were loaded onto a train, shipped back to Natal, and put into prison camps.

The march had gained the attention of England and India. The Viceroy in India and even the Parliament in London were appalled to hear that thousands of their subjects, including many children, were sentenced to hard labor in prison camps. By the time Gandhi was released from prison, a commission of inquiry had been established. But the commission had no Indian members, and some people on it were blatantly anti-Indian. Even though he had just completed a long prison term, Gandhi announced a march against the commission.

Just before that march was to start, however, the South African railroad workers, who were white and had nothing to do with *satyagraha,* went on strike. The strike became so serious and widespread that it threatened General Botha's position as Prime Minister of South Africa. Gandhi could have exploited this situation to further his cause. But wanting neither to oust the Botha government nor confuse the Indian and railroad issues, Gandhi called off the march.

Prime Minister Botha and General Smuts were very impressed with Gandhi's decision. Though he represented no government and held no official office, they decided to negotiate with him as an equal. In June 1914, they abolished the head-tax on indentured laborers who purchased their freedom, and accepted the solemn validity of all Indian marriages. Indians were still not permitted to move freely between South African provinces, but Gandhi considered the compromise a victory for the *satyagraha* movement.

Two weeks later, Gandhi left South Africa. General Smuts expressed his respect for Gandhi succinctly: "The saint has left our shores," he said, "I hope forever."

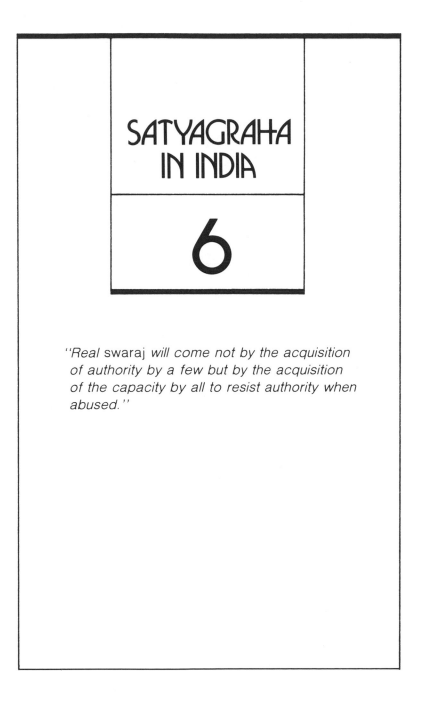

# SATYAGRAHA
# IN INDIA

# 6

"*Real* swaraj *will come not by the acquisition of authority by a few but by the acquisition of the capacity by all to resist authority when abused.*"

Before returning to India, Gandhi sailed to London, arriving in August 1914, just after World War I broke out. Though some friends there urged him to use England's problem to India's advantage, he once again displayed his loyalty by organizing an ambulance corps. The corps never made it to the battle-front, however, and Gandhi's stay in London was of little value except for some good advice he received from a friend, Gopal Krishna Gokhale, who had often visited Gandhi in South Africa.

Gokhale, a congressman in the Indian National Congress, was actively pushing for Indian independence. Gandhi showed him a manifesto he had written entitled *Hind Swaraj,* or *Home Rule.* The pamphlet advocated semi-independence, with Indians ruling themselves while maintaining close connections with the mother country, much as Canada and Australia did. It also outlined a socio-economic system similar to that of ancient India. Large industries would be replaced by cottage industries. The structure of the caste system would continue for the sake of social organization. Railroads would be abolished because walking was better for both body and soul. Moslem and Hindu traditions and taboos would be respected by all, including foreigners. In short, Gandhi wanted India to regress in order to rediscover its soul that England had all but destroyed.

Gokhale said that Indian social and political awareness had changed a lot during Gandhi's twenty years in South Africa. He suggested that Gandhi travel for a year before he expressed any political thoughts.

When Gandhi docked in Bombay in January 1915, he found that India had not changed as much as Gokhale had claimed. The untouchables were still living off garbage and dying as they slept in the streets. Latrines were covered with maggots and lice. Holy temples reeked with filth while their priests, above manual labor, solicited money from worshippers. The holy Ganges River, an important place of pilgrimage for Hindus, stank with human waste. Moslems and Hindus still hated each other.

Convinced that India did not deserve independence until living conditions improved, Mohandas and Kasturbai decided to establish a model community near the city of Ahmedabad in his native region of Gujarat on the Kathiawar peninsula. They called the community Sabarmati Ashram. Sabarmati was the nearby river; *ashram* was a kind of retreat where devout people lived while preparing their souls for death and reincarnation.

The *ashram* would follow the guidelines of the Phoenix and Tolstoy Farms, but would go one step further. It would accept Untouchables as members.

The introduction of an Untouchable family almost brought an end to the *ashram*. Several members, including Kasturbai, objected. The owner of the land did not want Untouchables polluting his well by drinking from it. Neighbors did not want Untouchables walking on their streets. The companies that were sponsoring the *ashram* did not want to be associated with the breaking of traditions that had stood for centuries.

Funds dried up. Some members left and many others refused to associate with the Untouchables. Unable to pay the rent, Gandhi prepared to move the *ashram* to an Untouchable slum inside Ahmedabad. But one day an anonymous Moslem drove up in a car, asked Gandhi if he needed money, handed him a sack of cash out the window, and drove off. The *ashram* was saved. Eventually, the Untouchables and the other members of the ashram learned to live together peacefully and harmoniously.

It was during this time that India's greatest living poet, the Nobel prizewinning Rabindranath Tagore, bestowed upon Gandhi the title of "Mahatma." Translated literally, it means Great Soul. Gandhi did not much like the title, but to Indian peasants it meant he was a veritable saint, so holy that merely being in his presence brought spiritual enrichment. To touch him, they said, would cure disease and ward off death. Gandhi consistently denied that he had any such mystical powers, and he refused to be considered any sort of God.

As Gokhale had advised, Gandhi waited a full year before raising his political voice. By then, he had seen enough and had plenty to say. His first opportunity to speak was the opening of the Hindu University in Benares. He had been invited by Mrs. Annie Besant, an Englishwoman who had founded the university and would later serve as a leader in the National Congress.

Wearing only the white cloak and *dhoti* loincloth of peasants, Gandhi sat on the speakers' platform among bemedaled English officials and Indian princes. Gandhi's clothing symbolized who he was and what he stood for. If the officials and students did not understand that, they certainly got the message from his speech.

Shouting with uncharacteristic anger, he scolded the university for hearing speeches in English rather than in an Indian language. He chided the officials for wearing expensive clothes and jewels that had been paid for with the sweat of peasants. He described India as he had seen it—filthy, impoverished, enslaved, and uneducated. He even went so far as to praise the courage, if not the tactics, of Indian militants who were daring to fight against what they thought was wrong.

As the officials began to walk out in protest, some students booed while others cheered. The ceremony broke up into rowdy chaos, leaving Gandhi with a reputation as a dangerous radical.


PEASANT POLITICS

Gandhi had an opportunity to put his words into action after a meeting of the National Congress in 1916. One of the subjects briefly debated was how English landlords were abusing tenant farmers in Champaran. But because the peasants of that rural area had no power, Congress was more interested in the urban problems of the educated population.

One peasant, however, saw hope in the Mahatma. After persistent pleas he managed to bring Gandhi to Champaran to observe the problems of his people.

The peasants did indeed have reason to complain. In the past, they had paid their rent with a share of their crops. But now the landlords were demanding impossible sums of money instead. While before the peasants had been merely without hope of owning their own land, now they were in danger of losing even the right to farm it. Lawyers whom the peasants had hired were being paid but were not producing results. They were suspected of secretly working for the landowners.

Gandhi took on the case, but as soon as he announced his intentions, local authorities ordered him to leave the district. He refused and quickly made arrangements for the *ashram* to continue his work if he were arrested. The next day he was in court pleading innocent to a charge of disturbing the peace, but admitting that he was guilty of disobeying the order to leave the district: "I have disregarded the order to leave not for lack of respect for local authority but in obedience to the higher law of our being, the voice of conscience."

The arrest made him a local hero. A jail sentence might incite riots or even a rebellion. So before local authorities could issue a sentence, the Viceroy in Delhi ordered his release.

Gandhi and his aides went from village to village to hear and record some seven thousand complaints from peasants. Wherever he went, joyous mobs surrounded the "liberator" Mahatma Gandhi. When he had enough evidence against the landowners, negotiations began under the arbitration of a special commission of inquiry. The landlords were required to repay part of the excessive rents and some illegal fees they had charged the peasants. The repayment was less than the peasants had hoped for, but enough to show that the English were admitting their guilt. Gandhi considered the negotiations successful because he had proven that the masses of poor people could be roused into action and that the government would bend, if not surrender, under pressure. Most important of all, the victory had come without violence.

FAST UNTO DEATH

In July 1917, the bubonic plague broke out in Ahmedabad, the hometown of the Sabarmati Ashram. As people fled the city, the local textile mill became short of workers. To induce the unskilled workers to stay or return, the mill offered them a 70 percent wage bonus.

Skilled workers, who did not receive the bonus, demanded a cost-of-living raise in order to meet price increases caused by World War I. Matters worsened when the plague abated and the 70 percent bonus was dropped. Unskilled workers joined skilled workers in their demand for a

50 percent raise in pay. The mill owners offered the ten thousand easily replaceable workers only 20 percent. Reconciliation seemed unlikely until both sides agreed to call on a mutually-respected arbitrator, the Mahatma of the local *ashram*. He was a champion of the poor, but at the same time he was grateful to the mill owners who had contributed large sums of money to the *ashram*. Having friends on both sides of the conflict, Gandhi hoped to guide them all toward the Truth.

The Truth proved hard to find. Gandhi suggested a compromise of a 35 percent pay raise. The owners refused. Some workers walked off their jobs. The owners then temporarily shut down the plant, giving everyone a taste of unemployment. The workers, who had been miserably poor beforehand, now faced hunger and greater hardship.

Gandhi then sided with the workers, but only after they agreed to remain nonviolent. They were not to harass any strikers who went back to work, and they were to remain firm in their commitment to the strike as long as necessary.

This was *satyagraha* with decent wages as its goal. Gandhi and the workers met under a large tree near the mill to make speeches and sing encouraging songs. The workers kept their promise to avoid violence, and in so doing won great respect from the people of Ahmedabad. And despite increasing hunger and poverty, the strikers did not lessen their demands.

The mill was re-opened. Some workers, seeing that their families were slowly starving, wanted to accept the owners' offer and return to work. Gandhi pleaded with them to hold out. *Satyagraha* takes time, he told them. But one worker made a speech saying that, of course, Gandhi was willing to hold out. He had money and plenty to eat and was given a car to ride to the tree every day.

"The light came to me," Gandhi later wrote. "Unbidden, the words came to my lips." The words were a vow not to eat until the owners agreed to the compromise increase or until the workers quit their jobs permanently. He would "fast unto death" if necessary.

Workers and owners alike were aghast. They knew the seriousness of Gandhi's vows. Workers offered to fast in his place, but he refused. The mill owners were under tremendous pressure. They could lose a man they dearly respected. And there was no telling what the workers would do if Gandhi died.

Gandhi had not wanted to blackmail the owners into settling the dispute. He had wanted them to agree voluntarily. Such was the principle of *satyagraha*. But they felt forced, and after three days of Gandhi's fast they agreed to the 35 percent raise.

After he had solved the Ahmedabad crisis, Gandhi responded to pleas for help in the nearby district of Kheda. The farmers there had suffered a terrible famine. The law said that when crop yields dropped below 25 percent of normal, farmers did not have to pay taxes. The British tax collectors, however, needed revenue for the war in Europe and claimed that the harvest was above the minimum.

Gandhi saw that, regardless of the war and the size of the harvest, the peasants were not able to pay. He told them not to fear the authorities and to refuse to pay the tax. The British responded by seizing crops and cattle. To protest, hundreds of upper-class Indians joined thousands of peasants in a march from village to village. Despite their intense anger, the Indians obeyed Gandhi's rule of nonviolence.

The British never officially canceled the tax, but they quietly stopped seizing crops and collected taxes only from those who could obviously afford it. Gandhi claimed a special victory; it was the first time upper-class and educated people had joined a *satyagraha*. Many of them would participate in future campaigns.

Gandhi and volunteers from the *ashram* stayed in Kheda a while longer to teach the farmers about home industry, cleanliness, and the importance of nonviolence. He called this education process his Constructive Program and would continue it throughout India the rest of his life.

In 1918, England needed more troops for the trenches of World War I. India had already supplied some eight hundred thousand, but Viceroy Chelmsford in Delhi wanted more. He called on Gandhi to find new recruits. Surprisingly, Gandhi agreed. He was still loyal to England, and he was counting on British fairmindedness to give India some degree of home rule in exchange for helping out in this time of need. Gandhi's critics later called this agreement a shrewd political move that contradicted his philosophy of nonviolence.

Certainly most Indians did not agree with Gandhi's decision. He returned to Kheda, walking from village to village hoping to get twenty recruits from each. But the people had not forgotten what the British had done to them.

When Gandhi had come to Kheda to fight the British, he had found open doors, free meals, and oxcarts to carry him and his aides. Now that he came to help the British, he had to sleep in fields and go hungry. He became seriously ill and returned to his *ashram*. Gandhi seemed to be sinking toward death. A doctor urged him to drink milk, but Gandhi had once vowed to his mother he would never do so. The doctor and Kasturbai finally convinced him to drink goat's milk, and he recovered. Although he was sure it tainted his soul, goat's milk became the only animal product he would consume. It would be part of his scanty meals ever after.

FROM NONVIOLENCE TO VIOLENCE

Though the battles of World War I never touched Indian soil, the country was wounded. Prices soared and high taxes drove millions into permanent poverty. A strike in Bombay involved some 125,000 workers. Epidemics of influenza and pneumonia killed 13 million. Incidents of terrorism became common. The Punjab region of northern India, always a violent area, rumbled with revolt. When the National Congress met in Delhi at the end of the war, its angry delegates called for revolution.

Because of the chaos, England declared that India was not ready for the independence Gandhi and the National Congress had been pressing for. Instead, the British restricted freedom to restore order. In February 1919, the Delhi government passed the Rowlatt Act, which allowed crimes against British rule to be tried in secret and without a jury. Such seditious acts included the possession of anti-British literature, a crime punishable by two years in prison. The Rowlatt Act also said that ten years hence, independence for India would be reconsidered.

The Rowlatt Act opposed everything Gandhi stood for. He felt betrayed by the country he had so consistently defended, but he didn't know how to react. A call for revolution would cause countless deaths. A nationwide *satyagraha* would be impossible to control. He decided to try another strategy, one never tried before: an all-India *hartal*, which is a general labor strike and day of prayer. This *hartal*, however, would last several days as a silent protest against the Rowlatt Act.

On April 16, 1919, all shops would close, and no cars or buses would move. No Indian would go to work. Everyone was to keep off the streets. All of India would fast and pray for freedom in the hope that the British would hear this silent message.

Almost all Indians, Moslems and Hindus alike, participated in the *hartal*, but many took to the streets chanting and carrying banners. Violence broke out. A train station and a bank were mobbed and destroyed; the British inside were literally torn to pieces. Government buildings were burned, trains were looted, and telegraph wires were cut.

In the Punjab city of Amritsar, an English schoolteacher was assaulted. Two days later British General Harry Dyer arrived to restore order. He banned all public meetings but failed to inform the public of this edict. On April 13, some five thousand Indians rallied in a plaza surrounded by buildings. Only a few alleyways served as entrances to or exits from the plaza, and these were suddenly blocked by troops. Following an order from General Dyer, the troops shot into the crowd with rifles until they ran out of ammunition. Out of 1,600 bullets, only 90 did not hit human flesh; 379 died and 1,137 lay wounded. No one was allowed to rescue them until the curfew ended the next day.

As punishment for the assault on the schoolteacher, all Indians in Amritsar were forced to crawl when they passed down her street. Those who didn't, including some children on their way to school, were flogged in public. For these and similar services to the British Empire, English citizens gave General Dyer a sword of honor and a special award of £27,000. The army pressured him into early retirement, however, for failing to understand his duties as an officer.

Gandhi blamed the violence of the British and the Indians on himself, calling it a "Himalayan blunder" to even attempt a national *hartal* or *satyagraha*. Sure that he should have known better than to trust either British civility or the discipline of masses of untrained *satyagrahis*, he fasted three days to punish himself.

It was clear that *satyagraha* would not work until people understood its principles. Gandhi saw that the National Congress could be a useful forum for teaching *satyagraha*. As its most respected advisor, he began to reorganize and give the Congress a new direction during 1920.

The Indian National Congress was not a governing body but rather a series of meetings held in various states. Until Gandhi took control, its members were almost exclusively upper-middle-class Indians who conversed and gave speeches in English, wore English clothes, had been educated in English schools, and in general seemed more devoted to joining the British than to ousting them. Meetings included bold speeches and revolutionary resolutions, but effective action was never taken.

Gandhi changed all that by drafting a new constitution. After 1920, anyone could become a member of the Congress by paying a paltry subscription fee of one-quarter of one rupee per year. The Moslem minority was encouraged to participate more actively. Gandhi's objective was to achieve an all-India policy of noncooperation with the British. This, said Gandhi, would bring *swaraj*, or home rule, within a year.

Noncooperation meant acting as if the British were nonexistent. Indian legal affairs would be conducted outside of British courts. Consumers would boycott British-made goods. Indian soldiers would abandon the British army. In a symbolic act, Gandhi kicked off the noncooperation campaign by giving back to the British the medal he had won in the Boer War in South Africa. He also shed and publicly burned his British-made cloak and turban, leaving himself only the *dhoti* loincloth, the "uniform" of the poorest of the Indian poor.

To spread the idea of a *satyagraha* of noncooperation throughout India, Gandhi organized the National Volunteer Corps, which was mostly made up of activist students. One of those young volunteers was Jawaharlal Nehru, the son of Motilal Nehru. Motilal Nehru, a prominent lawyer, was president of the Indian National Congress and was constantly at amiable odds with Gandhi. Nevertheless, he would inevitably support Gandhi in his various political projects. Jawaharlal often traveled with Gandhi as he toured the country to explain *satyagraha* and noncooperation.

A major goal in the struggle toward freedom was independence from the need for imported British textiles. As part of Gandhi's Constructive Program, the National Volunteers taught peasants how to weave their own clothes. They even invented a simple, compact spinning wheel so that anyone could turn raw cotten into finished clothing. This spinning wheel became a symbol of Indian nationalism and the nonviolent revolution. Gandhi would spin for at least half an hour a day, and gained great peace of mind from the methodical work. His spinning wheel would accompany him everywhere, from prison cells to the halls of Parliament.

At first the British did not fear the noncooperation campaign. But soon it began to disrupt their administrative and economic control. They began arresting congressional leaders and National Volunteers, including the entire Nehru family. By March 1920, some thirty thousand had been imprisoned. Mahatma Gandhi himself was arrested and put on trial.

He was charged with sedition for writing three especially inflammatory articles in *Young India*, a weekly magazine he had been editing for the past year. At his trial he pleaded guilty. In a moving testimony, he said, "I submit to the highest penalty that can be inflicted on me for what in law is a deliberate crime and what appears to me the highest duty of a citizen."

He then read a statement detailing all that England had done to India, and all that he and India had done for England. The judge was touched, but after expressing his respect for Gandhi, he declared that crime was crime and that the criminal would have to be punished. He sentenced Gandhi to six years, but added that he hoped the government would find some way to reduce that sentence.

Gandhi spent almost two years in prison. He meditated, read, wrote, and spinned thread. In December 1923 he was struck by appendicitis. On religious grounds, he refused surgery until the viceroy told him that if he died, India would rise up in a very bloody and poorly planned revolt. Gandhi submitted to the surgeon's scalpel, was saved, and then released from prison in February 1924.

Meanwhile, the *swaraj* movement had deteriorated into a contest between Hindus and Moslems. The Moslem League, organized by Mohammed Ali Jinnah, was not cooperating with the National Congress. Jinnah, born of Moslem parents, had studied law in London. But unlike Gandhi, Jinnah abandoned most of his religious beliefs and adopted English customs. He drank and smoked, wore the most dapper English clothes, and even used a monocle he didn't really need.

Except when it seemed politically wise, he was rarely seen inside a mosque.

After leaving Congress in 1920, Jinnah devoted himself to separating Moslems from Hindus. He feared that, in a democracy, the Hindu majority would mistreat the Moslem minority. Moslems readily believed this in spite of Gandhi's policy respecting all religions. It was most ironic that Gandhi, who was deeply religious, wanted a government that had no special allowances for different religions. Jinnah, a man who had little respect even for his own religion, wanted an Indian government that made special provisions for Moslems.

As Jinnah spread the fear that Hindus would one day enslave Moslems, Hindu–Moslem tensions built up. To Gandhi, this was a more serious problem than British rule. When rioting broke out in the Northwest Frontier Province, Gandhi vowed to fast for twenty-one days, or until his death, or until Hindu–Moslem relations improved.

Not long after news of the fast spread, Hindus and Moslems stopped fighting and demonstrated their unity in the streets. Mixed groups came to Gandhi's bed to swear that they would be friends. Gandhi's fast, later known as The Great Fast, lasted the full twenty-one days. Moslem–Hindu unity would last only a couple of years.

For the next five years, Gandhi concentrated primarily on his Constructive Program and social reform. He toured the country to preach the spiritual and economic importance of spinning and weaving, of Hindu–Moslem understanding, and of the acceptance of Untouchables as part of society.

With him went a most ardent and unusual apostle. She was called Mirabehn ("Aunt Mira"), but had been born Madeline Slade, the daughter of a British admiral. When she read of Gandhi, she went to India to join him at Sabarmati Ashram. She shaved her head and wore the simple *sari* dress of Indian women. She respected Gandhi almost as a god, serving his every need and following him everywhere as a disciple, nurse, secretary, and envoy.

Mirabehn was not the only person who revered Gandhi. Wherever he went, tens of thousands would stampede for a chance to touch him or kiss his feet. Gandhi once saw a man with a picture of the Mahatma hanging from his neck. The man claimed that he had been cured of paralysis by whispering "Gandhi, Gandhi," over and over. Gandhi told him, "It was not I who cured you. It was God."

After years of traveling and preaching, he felt that at last India understood the nature of *satyagraha*. In 1928 he stepped back into politics with a *satyagraha* of civil disobedience in Bardoli, in the Gujarat region. The peasants there were to disobey a 22 percent tax increase by refusing to pay. To Gandhi's delight, the *satyagrahis* remained peaceful as the government arrested them in great numbers and seized their property. The jails filled up and the government backed down. The prisoners were released, property was returned, and the tax increase was repealed. Civil disobedience had worked.

THE SALT MARCH

In 1919, with the passing of the infamous Rowlatt Act, Britain had agreed to reconsider the possibility of Indian independence in 1929. By 1927, however, the National Congress thought itself ready to rule India. With tumultuous in-house political maneuvering, they debated whether independence should be total and immediate or gradual, preceded by a dominion status similar to that of Canada and Australia.

To investigate the possibility of independence, England established a special commission. But since the commission failed to include any Indians, the National Congress boycotted it and set up its own commission with Motilal Nehru as its chairman. They drafted a constitution but Mohammed Ali Jinnah, who had been out of the country at the time, claimed that the Moslem League had not been properly consulted. Jinnah declared the constitution invalid since it did not represent all of India. He demanded some fourteen major changes before he would accept it.

To help resolve this conflict and indecision, Congress called Mahatma Gandhi to its December 1928 meeting in Calcutta. There Gandhi simply declared that if India was not given at least dominion status within one year, he would begin a nationwide *satyagraha*.

On January 1, 1930, Jawaharlal Nehru took office as president of Congress. His first act in that office was to read a Declaration of Independence and unfurl the flag of free India.

This flag alone by no means meant independence was achieved. It was a bold beginning but further action needed to be taken. That second, more difficult, step they left up to Gandhi.

It took two full months for "an inner voice" to tell him what to do. On March 2, 1930, he wrote a long letter to the Viceroy, Lord Irwin. He said that he "held British rule to be a curse" and told him why: "It has impoverished dumb millions by a system of progressive exploitation and by a ruinous, expensive military and civil administration which the country could never afford. It has reduced us politically to serfdom. It has sapped the foundations of our culture. And it has degraded us spiritually."

And then he said what he would do about it: "On the eleventh day of this month, I shall proceed to disregard the Salt Law."

The Viceroy's answer was a cold, curt letter from his secretary warning Gandhi not to disobey the law. Gandhi's response: "On bended knee I asked for bread, and I received stone instead."

Obviously the Viceroy was not worried. The Salt Law was a taxation on all salt and a prohibition against the making, selling, or eating of any salt not imported from England. Gandhi thought that since salt was a necessity of life and since it lay in God-given plentitude along the beaches of India,

Gandhi (center) and his followers
march to the Arabian Sea, where they
broke the English Salt Law.

it was criminal that an impoverished people be required by law to buy it. Viceroy Irwin thought Gandhi's protest ridiculous.

The Viceroy was wrong; the protest was ingenious. On March 12, a scrawny, half-naked sixty-year-old man began a 200-mile (322-km) march from Sabartami Ashram to the coastal town of Dandi. He left with a few disciples, including young Jawaharlal Nehru, and several journalists. Walking 12 miles (20 km) a day, they gathered hundreds of followers from every village they passed through. Peasants sprinkled water on the road to keep the dust down, and scattered leaves and flower petals to ease the way for bare feet.

At night the marchers stopped to pray, to discuss the importance of what they were doing, and to sleep. "We are marching in the name of God," Gandhi told them. They read the New Testament aloud and began to see the similarities between their march and Jesus' journey to Jerusalem. Gandhi had a feeling he might meet his death at the end of his trek. The day before they arrived at the beach, he said, "Either I shall return with what I want, or else my dead body will float in the ocean."

On April 6, 1930, Mahatma Gandhi waded into the Arabian Sea, performed a Hindu purification ritual, picked up a bit of salt from the sand, and ate it. As simply as that, the Salt Law was broken.

Within days, the whole world knew what he had done. Thousands of Indians flocked to the beaches to scoop up sea water in shallow pans, let it evaporate, and scrape off the salt that remained. They saw that what Gandhi had done to the Salt Law they could do to all similar laws. They boycotted all English goods and set up picket lines around shops that sold British textiles. As fast as the police could beat up and haul away the passive picketers, new ones would join the protests.

The British government in Delhi waited a month to see if the excitement would die down. It didn't. On May 4, they arrested Gandhi as he slept under a mango tree near Dandi. Since it was his day of silence, he submitted without a word. He was imprisoned without charges and without a trial, and was held "at the pleasure of the government" under an all-but-forgotten law of 1827. Elsewhere, Nehru and other leaders were arrested.

Gandhi could have asked for nothing more. Once again he was a martyr. And this time, he knew his people were prepared to carry out a peaceful *satyagraha*.

Three weeks later, twenty-five hundred National Volunteers massed for a raid on the Dharasana Saltworks. They were led by Mrs. Sarojini Naidu, one of India's foremost poets and, while Nehru was in prison, acting-president of the Congress. The volunteers faced a defending force of four hundred Indian police armed with the wicked iron-tipped bamboo clubs called *lathis*. United Press reporter Webb Miller witnessed the action:

> In complete silence, the Gandhi men drew up and halted a hundred yards from the stockade. A picked column advanced from the crowd, waded the ditches, and approached the barbed-wire stockade. . . . Suddenly, at a word of command, scores of native policemen rushed upon the advancing marchers and rained blows on their heads with their steel-shod *lathis*. Not one of the marchers even raised an arm to fend off the blows. They went down like tenpins. From where I stood, I heard the sickening wack of the clubs on unprotected skulls. The waiting crowd of marchers groaned and sucked in their breath in sympathetic pain at every blow. Those struck down fell sprawling, unconscious or writhing with fractured skulls or broken shoulders. . . . The survivors, without breaking ranks, silent and doggedly marched on until struck down. . . .

They marched steadily, with heads up, without the encouragement of music or cheering or any possibility that they might escape serious injury or death. The police rushed out and methodically and mechanically beat down the second column. There was no fight, no struggle; the marchers simply walked forward until struck down.

The Saltworks was saved, but the whole world heard about the incident.

In early 1931, Gandhi and other leaders of Congress were released from prison. Motilal Nehru died a few days later, but his son, Jawaharlal, and Gandhi were eager to join the battle again. At Viceroy Irwin's request, Gandhi agreed to negotiate an end to the *satyagraha*. Irwin was also hoping to interest Gandhi in attending the Second Round Table Conference to be held in London in May. The First Round Table Conference had taken place while Gandhi was in prison. No one from the National Congress had attended, although the Moslem League and other factions had had representatives there.

Beginning on February 16, 1931, Gandhi and Irwin met eight times. Apparently Gandhi was quite a sight, arriving on foot and bounding up the steps of the Viceroy's opulent pink palace.

In England, Winston Churchill disdainfully remarked: "It is nauseating to see Mr. Gandhi, a seditious lawyer, now posing as fakir, striding half-naked up the steps of the palace, while he is still organizing and conducting a defiant campaign of civil disobedience, to parley on equal terms with the representative of the King-Emperor."

In what Congress later ratified as The Delhi Pact, Gandhi agreed to stop the *satyagraha* if Irwin would release all non-violent prisoners, allow Indians onto the coast to collect salt from the beaches, and return confiscated property. Although the concessions were far less than the independence Gandhi

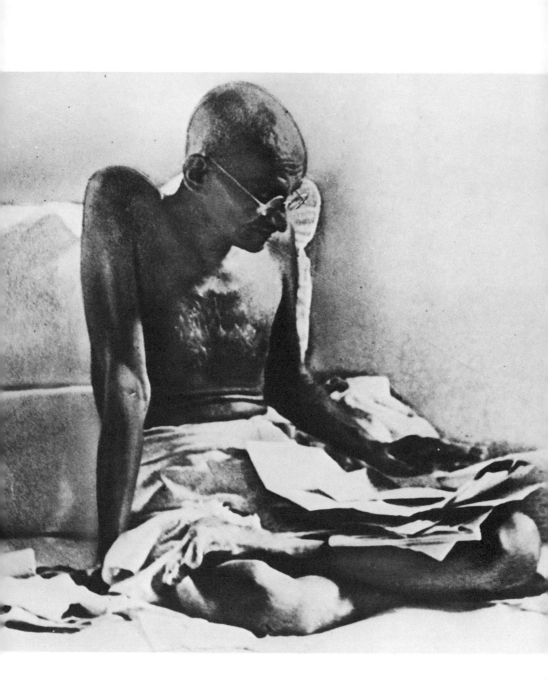

*Mahatma Gandhi just after completing his prison term for disobeying the English Salt Law.*

had demanded in the beginning, he felt it was most significant that the viceroy was now negotiating rather than issuing incontestable orders.

The pact did not last long, however. Lord Irwin was replaced by Lord Willingdon, who had little respect for either Gandhi or the pact signed by his predecessor. To negotiate with him, Gandhi traveled by train to the British summer capital of Simla, in the foothills of the Himalayas. There Viceroy Willingdon denied him the use of a government car, suggesting that Gandhi hire a man-powered rickshaw for the 6-mile (10-km) commute from a friend's house to the palace. To that Gandhi said, "I will never allow my brother men to become beasts of burden for me. I will walk."

And walk he did, at the age of sixty-one, up and down hills, through chilly rain, 12 miles (20 km) a day, for negotiations that yielded nothing.

Gandhi was supposed to leave for the Round Table Talks in London on May 22, 1931. London had reserved special cabins on a boat for him and the other delegates. But Gandhi wasn't ready. Before he could negotiate in London, he needed to know that Congress would stand behind whatever he did there, and that Hindus and Moslems would not argue about whatever he agreed to.

Earlier in March, he had reluctantly agreed that Moslems could have separate elections for their representatives to Congress. The plan would guarantee them one-third of the seats, even though they comprised only one-quarter of India's population. Gandhi had hoped that this extra concession would keep the Moslems happy, but they began to quarrel among themselves about the desirability of separate elections. Gandhi did not want to even try to settle that matter, so he left for London with a divided and subdivided India behind him and not much hope for independence ahead of him.

At the time, England was suffering from rising unemployment, an increasing national debt, and the rapid decline of the Brit-

*While traveling to England to attend the
Indian Round Table Conference (facing page),
Gandhi spins threads aboard the English Channel
steamer* Biarritz. *Above:* the Indian Round
Table Conference in London, in 1931, where Gandhi
*unsuccessfully demanded independence for India.*

ish pound. As Gandhi toured the slums of London, the poor people there cheered him. He told them he was saddened to see that so many textile mills had laid off their workers and gone bankrupt because India had so successfully boycotted imported textiles. When he sat at the Round Table Conference, he used this poverty in his argument for independence.

"India has been held by the sword," he told the attending members of Parliament. "But which would be better—an enslaved but rebellious India or an India as an esteemed partner? . . . Perchance it may be possible for India to be a valuable partner, not held by force but by the silken cord of love. I have come here in a spirit of cooperation."

He was demanding total independence but expecting nothing. The other Indian delegates were of little help, apparently desiring little more than to get their names in *The Times* of London. By the end of the conference, Hindus and Moslems were openly arguing and insulting each other during the meetings. They seemed to be proving what the British had been claiming all along—that Indians were not yet capable of governing themselves. When the conference fizzled to an end on October 8, 1931, Gandhi declared, "This has been the most humiliating day of my life." A few days later he left London for the last time, returning to India exhausted, discouraged, and empty-handed.

# HAI RAMA!

# 7

"Man is the maker of his own destiny in the
sense that he has the freedom of choice
as to the manner in which he uses his own
freedom. But he is no controller of results."

When Viceroy Willingdon learned of the failure of the Round Table Conference, he foresaw trouble. To prevent the organization of another civil disobedience campaign, he arrested all active leaders of the National Congress. By the time Gandhi's boat arrived in India on December 28, 1931, the independence movement was paralyzed. Gandhi begged the Viceroy to meet with him, but Willingdon refused. Gandhi realized that civil disobedience had to be launched again.

"The government has flagrantly broken the Delhi Pact," he told Congress. "The nation must respond to the challenge."

The next day, January 4, 1932, he was arrested without charges or a trial and sent to Yeravda Jail in Poona, a small city near Bombay. Congress was outlawed. Within two months, 35,000 of its members were behind bars. The independence movement was all but dead, but Mahatma Gandhi was still alive.

Not one to let iron bars put him out of action, he took on

the cause of the Untouchables in a way that surprised everyone.

London was establishing the right of Untouchables to have separate elections in the provinicial, or local, assemblies. Dr. Bhimrao Ramji Ambedkar, the leader of the Untouchable political party, was hoping to adopt the same rule into the Indian constitution one day. This would guarantee the Untouchables a certain number of seats in these provincial governments. Without such a rule, the more numerous casted Hindus would be able to vote the outcastes out of the government. On the surface it seemed a fair proposition, but Gandhi opposed it. He did not want the constitution to specifically segregate the Untouchables from the rest of society. To prevent legalized electoral segregation, he began another fast unto death.

Doctors warned that he was too old for another fast, that at the age of sixty-three, three weeks without food would quite likely put him in a coma that food could not cure. Gandhi said he would let God decide if he lived or died, but London and Dr. Ambedkar felt the decision was up to them. After seven days of negotiations in Yeravda Jail and frantic telegrams to and from London, a compromise was reached. The Untouchables would have separate primary elections for 18 percent of the assembly seats and then would participate in the general elections. The difference between this and the original proposition was slight. The success was of a sort few understood. Because of the extraordinarily emotional means of achieving it, India did not interpret it as a compromise with the British but rather a victory over them. As a result, India saw new value in its poorest citizens. Holy temples and schools were opened to them and monies were raised for their education.

Gandhi spent his next several months at Yeravda writing articles for the magazine *Harijan*, which was dedicated to correcting the evils of the caste system. But the more he wrote, the more he felt personally guilty for the sins of Hinduism. In

May 1933, to punish himself for these sins, he began another twenty-one-day fast.

No one believed he would survive. The seven-day fast of the year before had almost killed him. How could he survive fasting three times as long?

As he grew weaker and weaker, the government feared he might die while in their hands. To avoid a dangerous public outcry, they released him. Miraculously, he lived through the fast and soon recuperated.

Meanwhile, Sabarmati Ashram was thriving. Over a hundred people lived there. Its fields and workshops were becoming valuable assets, so valuable that the British thought them worthy of taxation. On Gandhi's orders, issued from Yeravda Jail, the ashramites refused to pay. This led to a seizure of portions of their crops and equipment. Upon his release, Gandhi proposed a peaceful solution. He told everyone to abandon the *ashram*. He instructed the members of the commune to go live among the peasants of a hundred villages, but not before staging a public protest first. Gandhi organized a march but was arrested before it began. He was sentenced to another year in prison.

This time he was not allowed to publish anything, not even a nonpolitical defense of the Untouchables. Again he started a fast. Again the government, afraid he was going to die, released him. Again he survived.

Without Sabarmati Ashram, Gandhi needed another place to live. He wanted to escape the pressures of the public and the political connections that had formed like a web around him. He chose the hamlet of Segaon. While Mirabehn saw to the building of a hut, he lived under a bamboo mat stretched between poles. That scant shelter was plenty for the leader of hundreds of millions of people, a man who quite likely could have had the Taj Mahal if he had asked for it. Such a man does not escape public attention merely by leaving the city. His retreat from the world only caused an endless flow of politicians, pilgrims, and reporters to walk that much farther to see him.

In 1935 the British government passed the Government of India Act that would, at last, replace the Rowlatt Act of 1919. The eleven Indian provinces, composed of over six hundred princely states, would be allowed to govern themselves with some degree of independence. A complicated election system would create provincial assemblies in which all religious, political, and caste factions would hold seats. The real power, however, would remain in Delhi, under British control.

The National Congress, with Jawaharlal Nehru as its president, was by no means satisfied with this form of government. Gandhi noted that India was still a prison but that now the prisoners were allowed to elect the officials who ran the prison. Congress hotly debated whether to participate in the elections. Without accepting the Government of India Act as anywhere near adequate, the Congress decided to let their own members seek office. By February 1937, they held a majority of seats in nine out of eleven provinces. The Moslem League had won only 5 percent of the Moslem vote. Dr. Ambedkar's candidates won only thirteen of the seventy-eight seats reserved for Untouchables.

Mohammed Ali Jinnah could not accept that he had virtually no support. In various speeches he predicted a "Hindu dictatorship" over the Moslems. Refusing to accept anything but a political system segregated by religion, he was beginning to raise a specter so ugly that it brought tears to Gandhi's eyes. The monster on the horizon was called Pakistan. Still just an idea, Jinnah envisioned it as an independent Moslem country created from the northwest and northeast areas of India, where Moslems were most heavily concentrated. East and West Pakistan would be a single country divided by 1,000 miles (1,600 km) of Indian territory. Each letter of its name stood for one area Pakistan would control. Together, the letters spelled the word that meant "land of the pure" in

the Farsi language of Iran and Afghanistan. Pakistan was Jinnah's dream and Gandhi's nightmare.

WORLD WAR II

With the German *blitzkrieg* invasion of Poland, World War II
began in Europe in September 1939. Gandhi was still
secluded in Segaon, which was now a successful commune
known as *Sevagram*, or "Service Village." Cut off from the
world, he apparently had little understanding of the European
situation. Perhaps his profound innocence prevented him
from seeing the sheer evil of Adolf Hitler and The Third Reich.
He wrote a "Dear Friend" letter to Hitler suggesting that, in
the name of peace and nonviolence, he call back his army.
He suggested that England resist with nonviolence, a tactic
he did not know was allowing the Nazis to round up and
slaughter millions of German and Polish Jews. Although he
saw the war as a battle between imperialist powers, he wept
at reports of German bombs and missiles falling on his
beloved London. Although the National Congress thought it a
strategic time to demand independence, Gandhi did not want
to take advantage of England's terrible situation.
  England had no such sympathies for India, however. To
keep the peace there, they once again restricted what little
freedom the Indians had. Another passive resistance movement was begun. Within a few days, Gandhi, Nehru, and
some four hundred other leaders were in prison. By 1941,
they were joined by twenty thousand protestors. But by
December of that year, the movement had died out. A few
days before the Japanese attack on Pearl Harbor, the leaders were released.
  The war against Japan hit closer to home. Burma and
China, both bordering on India, were invaded. Gandhi agreed
with the decision of Nehru and Congress to contribute to
England's war effort, but only as a free nation. London
offered India a dominion status after the war. But the propo-

sition did not allow India to become fully independent if and when India so desired. It also would have allowed any province, princely state, or religious group to secede and form its own nation. Theoretically, India could have broken up into over five hundred different countries.

Gandhi refused London's offer and issued his strongest demand yet: "Quit India." The slogan meant that he wanted the British government and forces out of India immediately, without conditions or postponements. The most he would offer was temporary use of Indian territory for the fight against Japan. Congress backed him and said that a free India would fight any Japanese invasion with arms as well as nonviolent noncooperation.

The next day, August 8, 1942, Gandhi and the officers of Congress were arrested again. In apparent deference to Gandhi's seventy-two years of age, Viceroy Linlithgow had him imprisoned at the Aga Khan's palace in Poona. In order to join him there, Kasturbai made an anti-British speech and was promptly arrested. A few other friends from Congress were also sent there.

India erupted in revolt. With most of the leaders of Congress in prison, there was no one to control or organize the uprising. Gandhi and Nehru, who had neither planned nor desired the violence, disavowed responsibility, laying the blame on the British. As they sat helpless in their palace prison, riotous throngs burned banks, post offices, and train stations. British police and tax collectors were killed. Telegraph lines were cut and trains were derailed. Some parts of India were completely cut off from Delhi. By the time the violence died down, over six hundred had been killed and thirty-six thousand imprisoned.

Famine spread. Over a million people starved to death. Not without reason, the people blamed British negligence. Fighting the Germans and the Japanese and putting down the rebellion had been more important than saving the lives of Indian peasants.

To protest his imprisonment and all the problems it was

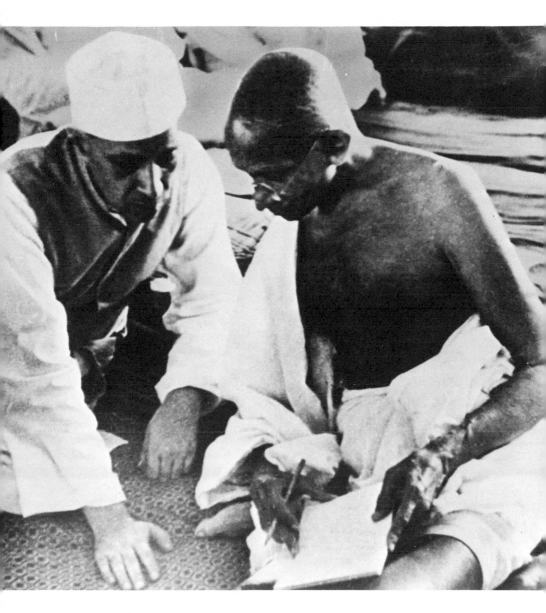

*Jawaharlal Nehru and Mahatma Gandhi during
the National Congress session in 1942 when
the "Quit India" resolution was adopted.*

*A nightly prayer meeting led by Gandhi in New Delhi, 1946.*

causing, Gandhi started another twenty-one-day fast on February 10, 1943. The newly-appointed Viceroy Wavell refused to release him or his prisonmates at the Aga Khan's palace. To keep him alive, Wavell sent doctors to care for him. Once again, Gandhi survived the fast.

Kasturbai was not as resilient. She became depressed in confinement. She experienced heart trouble, and then bronchitis. Gandhi refused to let doctors give her penicillin injections. On February 22, 1944, as her head lay in her husband's lap, her breathing stopped short. Gandhi asked, "What is it?" She gasped, "I don't know what it is," and died.

Six weeks later Gandhi had a malaria attack, his temperature reaching 105 degrees. After the fever came down, he was infected with hookworm and amoebic dysentery. Doctors advised the Viceroy to let him die elsewhere. On May 6, 1944, Gandhi left imprisonment for the last time. During the seventy-five years of his life, he had spent 2,338 days in prison. In the few years of freedom left to him, Gandhi still had much to do.

During World War II, Mohammed Ali Jinnah observed the tactics of Adolf Hitler. He sensed that he could manipulate the Indian situation to his own advantage. Assuming the Moslem title of *Quaid-e-azam*, or Great Leader — similar to Hitler's title of *Fuhrer* — Jinnah offered to return the Moslems to their former greatness when Islam's armies conquered the Mideast, north Africa, and parts of Asia, and for a while ruled over the Indian Hindus. To build political support, he found ambitious men and promised them political office in the Pakistan he was planning. To foster popular support, he told Moslems they would suffer humility and slavery if they stayed in India under Hindu rule.

The British were preparing to give India its independence at the end of World War II. Gandhi attempted to negotiate with Jinnah, but the Moslem was determined to create his own country. As Britain made ready to pull out, the Moslem League tried to wedge into the power vacuum. Moslem death squads terrorized Hindus by murdering their leaders and burning homes and temples. Vengeful Hindu death squads responded in kind. Riots broke out in Bombay, Calcutta, and Madras. In Calcutta alone, five thousand people were killed after five days of fighting.

In February 1947, Lord Louis Mountbatten became viceroy. Mountbatten's assignment was to complete the British pullout from India by August. Jinnah delivered an ultimatum to Congress: if an independent Pakistan was not created, there would be civil war. Congress had no choice but to give Jinnah the territories he wanted. Two separate areas in northwest and northeast India became Pakistan.

The concession to the Moslems was like the touch of a match to a powder keg. On August 13, two days before Independence Day, Gandhi arrived in Calcutta hoping to prevent more riots. But even some Hindus had turned against him, claiming that he had betrayed them. Rioters swarmed around the Moslem home where he was staying. There were reports of outright civil war from the Punjab area that bordered Pakistan. Hindus were fleeing Pakistan; Moslems were fleeing India. Fighting between them was satanic. Entire trainloads of people were massacred. An estimated half a million people died while trying to get into or out of Pakistan. Fifteen million lost their homes.

To stop what could only be described as mass madness, Gandhi once again offered his life. He began another fast unto death. He was now seventy-seven years old.

The riots continued for a while but soon the Hindus began to fear that their beloved leader would die. Moslems, realizing that they would be blamed for his death, agreed to stop fighting. Hindus and Moslems began to parade together to call their comrades to unity. Gandhi was encouraged but still not convinced. Finally, four days into the fast, when death squads from both sides came to his bed to drop their weapons and end their fighting. Gandhi began to eat again. Free India was two weeks old.

Having barely recovered his strength, Gandhi returned to Delhi, hoping to go on to Punjab. But in Delhi, horrendous conditions forced him to stop. Every mosque had been plundered. Most of the Moslem districts had been burned to the ground. Dead bodies lay in the streets. Millions of refugees, most penniless and hungry, filled the streets and alleys with tents. Cholera and smallpox raged out of control, killing thousands each day. Government was virtually nonexistent.

Gandhi wanted to stay in an *ashram* in a Delhi slum, but it was filled with refugees. Instead, he stayed at the mansion of a rich friend. There he conferred with Nehru and other leaders, desperately searching for a solution. In the garden of the mansion, he held prayer meetings for Hindus and Moslems alike. Although he was still weak from his fast, he went to preach nonviolence in refugee camps, some of which held up to seventy-five thousand people. As he tried to reason with the crowds, sporadic chants of "Death to Gandhi" revealed the depth of their discontent.

Shortly after his seventy-eighth birthday, he saw that his efforts to reason with the people were failing. It seemed that only fasting worked, so he began another fast on January 13, 1948. This time his condition deteriorated rapidly. As he made appeals for peace over the radio, all India could hear that his voice was growing weaker every hour. Bulletins reported every sip of water, every lost pound, every cramp, and eventually the failure of his kidneys. When he became too weak to continue the prayer sessions in the garden, Hindus and Moslems once again declared their brotherhood. People marched in the streets and leaders from both religions gathered around Gandhi's bed. On January 18, 1948 when Gandhi took his first sip of orange juice, Delhi and most of India was at peace.

Following the Delhi fast, Gandhi planned a mass march to Pakistan as soon as he regained his strength. For several days, friends had to carry him in a chair to his prayer sessions. Hundreds of people waited to hear him in the garden every evening.

On January 20, a bomb exploded during Gandhi's prayers. The young man who threw it was captured. Interrogation revealed a conspiracy by radical Hindus who wanted to kill the man who had called Moslems their brothers—the man who had allowed Moslems to take a large piece of India as their own. But the would-be assassin did not reveal the names of his coconspirators.

Gandhi was not afraid. "If I die by the bullet of a madman," he said, "I must do so smiling. Should such a thing happen to me, you are not to shed one tear."

Refusing to be called anything more than merely human, he told his grandniece, ". . . if someone shot at me and I received his bullet in my bare chest without a sign and with Rama's [God's] name on my lips, only then should you say that I was a true Mahatma."

The next day, January 30, 1948, as the Mahatma walked through the garden to his evening prayers, a Hindu named Nathuram Godse pushed through the crowd and dived to kiss Gandhi's feet. As he was pulled up, he leaned back, pointed a handgun at Gandhi and shot him three times in the abdomen and chest. Gandhi fell to the ground and breathed his last words: "Hai Rama!"—O God!

AFTER GANDHI

Mohammed Ali Jinnah became governor-general of East and West Pakistan but died in 1948 of a lung disease he had contracted years before. In 1970 an East Pakistani was elected president, but military leaders in West Pakistan refused to let him take office. Early in 1971, East Pakistan declared itself an independent country called Bangladesh. When troops from West Pakistan tried to take control over the insurgent half of the country, fierce battles resulted in the deaths of a million people and mass starvation ensued. Some ten million

Gandhi's ashes are carried to the
holy Ganges River for immersion.

refugees fled into India. India sent military aid to Bangladesh and, in December 1971, attacked Pakistan on both eastern and western fronts. After a few weeks of fighting, West Pakistan granted independence to Bangladesh and ended the war against India.

Jawaharlal Nehru continued as prime minister of India until his death in 1964. During his leadership he worked to build what he called a Socialist Society. This was by no means a brand of Soviet or Chinese socialism. Democracy and capitalistic principles were preserved as many important industries were put under government control, education was improved, cottage industries were developed, and large land holdings were redistributed among peasants. The caste system no longer existed in the eyes of the government, although it remained very much a part of the Indian social structure. Regardless of social attitudes, however, Untouchables today have the same constitutional rights as all other Indians.

In 1966 Nehru's daughter, Indira Gandhi, was elected prime minister. That she shares the Mahatma's name yet is not related to him has been called one of the great ironies of history; her political philosophy has had little respect for democracy and the hard-won Indian constitution. In 1975, when opposing political parties threatened her position, she declared a national emergency which gave her the constitutional right to dictatorial powers. She claimed the measure was necessary because of India's collapsing economy and widespread labor strikes and riots. Freedom of the press was curtailed and thousands of her opponents were arrested. Opposing political parties, feeling she was abusing her powers, formed a coalition, and by parliamentary vote they ousted her from office in 1977. That coalition did not manage to achieve much else, however. The situation in India steadily grew worse, and in 1980 Mrs. Gandhi was reelected prime minister.

Under Mrs. Gandhi's leadership, India developed strong ties with both the Soviet Union and the United States. U.S. technology helped India build its first nuclear power plant in

1970. In May 1974 India exploded an underground nuclear device, but none have been detonated since. In April 1979 the Soviet Union launched an Indian satellite into orbit. Mrs. Gandhi visited both President Reagan and Premier Breshnev in 1982, hoping to continue ties with both.

## SATYAGRAHA IN AMERICA

Mahatma Gandhi died but his Truth did not. His code of non-violence lives on. It is seen again and again around the world like a soul reborn in the womb of social injustice. Just as Gandhi's inner voice told him what was right and wrong, non-violent resistance movements have reminded humanity that its various societies are not yet pure and perfect. The United States has given birth to its share of justifiable *satyagrahis* and surely will see more in the future.

Finally, we look at a great American and his nonviolent efforts to correct democracy's shortcomings. At first backed by a minority, his shout was but a whisper in the American ear. But he was wielding the force of the Truth.

## MARTIN LUTHER KING, JR.

On January 15, 1929, Martin Luther King, Jr. was born in Atlanta, Georgia. Though a citizen of a nation renowned for its freedom, he—as all other blacks in that part of the country—was a second-class citizen. Had the locale been South Africa, he would have been called a "coolie." Had it been India, he would have been an Untouchable. But this was America, so he was called a "nigger."

He and other blacks had to drink from separate fountains, use separate soda machines, eat in separate restaurants, study in separate schools, worship in separate churches, sleep in separate hotels, live in separate neighborhoods, and sit in separate seats on public buses.

One December day in 1955, a tired black seamstress named Rosa Parks boarded such a segregated bus and took a seat in the fifth row. Soon the bus filled and, as a few whites were standing in the aisle, the bus driver ordered Mrs. Parks to give her seat to a white man. By law, this was a white person's right. But Mrs. Parks was exhausted from working all day. When she refused to get up, a police officer arrested her, took her to the police station, and charged her with violating the city's segregation code.

As fate would have it, a local Baptist minister named Martin Luther King, Jr. was inspired by the incident. A few years earlier he had attended a lecture by a man who had traveled to India. The man talked about a most fascinating revolutionary leader there, Mahatma Gandhi. King, a theology student at the time, saw the divine beauty of *satyagraha*. Its Christian-like tactics were passive and loving. *Satyagraha* integrated religion with politics in the name of justice and equality. King believed a passive resistance movement was the way to fight unjust discrimination against blacks. The case of Rosa Parks was a good place to start.

The first black American passive resistance movement was a boycott of the public buses in Montgomery, Alabama. Dr. King urged Montgomery blacks to keep their protest peaceful. "There will be no threats and no intimidations," he told them at a meeting in his church. "We will be guided by the highest principles of law and order. Our method will be that of persuasion, not coercion. We will only say to the people: 'Let your conscience be your guide.' "

To ensure that his *satyagrahis* could withstand the punishment that no doubt awaited them, they held role-playing sessions, teaching the boycotters not to fight back or curse attackers.

Those who opposed the boycott were not peaceful. The Ku Klux Klan and white "citizens' councils" terrorized blacks. Employers threatened to fire blacks who did not ride the bus to work. Dr. King's house was bombed, as were the homes of many other blacks. As Mahatma Gandhi would have predicted, the violence of oppressors directed national attention to Montgomery, and the passivity of its oppressed people awakened the national conscience. In November 1956, the United States Supreme Court declared that segregation on public buses was unconstitutional. Passive resistance had worked in Montgomery, and Dr. Martin Luther King, Jr. knew it could free his people all over America.

In the summer of 1957 Ranganath Diwaker, a disciple of Gandhi, flew from India to Alabama to talk with the leader of America's nonviolent movement. Diwakar advised King to follow Gandhi more closely by accepting more personal suffering. While King would not go so far as to fast unto death, he saw the wisdom in allowing himself to be arrested and then refusing to be released on bail. This tactic could create even more sympathy for his cause. He would be arrested many times, often for such petty crimes as minor traffic infractions.

People began to compare King to Gandhi. In 1958 a mentally deranged woman stabbed Dr. King while he was autographing books in a Harlem department store. Upon regaining consciousness, his first concern was that the would-be assassin be put in a hospital and not a prison cell.

The following year Dr. King and his wife, Coretta, went to India to learn more about Gandhi. There they saw that India was still deeply divided by caste and religion. Dr. King thought it most significant that, although Gandhi and his followers had adhered to the principle of nonviolence, their movement had actually caused much violence. The same problem could easily afflict the movement in America.

Several organizations were starting civil disobedience campaigns in the South. One of the most active was the Student Nonviolent Coordinating Committee (SNCC). SNCC became famous for its sit-ins in places that did not allow blacks. The students, blacks as well as whites, would first advise the management of a store or restaurant that segregation was morally wrong. If the management refused to change its policies, a group of students would sit somewhere on the premises and refuse to move until arrested. They followed a strict code of behavior that prohibited violent words or actions. They were courteous at all times and passively noncooperative when arrested. They were taught to remember that they were trying to overcome evil, not the evil-doers.

Another civil rights organization, the Congress of Racial Equality (CORE), led by James Farmer, initiated what they called Freedom Rides. With students from SNCC they rode in interstate buses across the South in 1961. At various stops they desegregated lunch counters and rest rooms by disregarding laws that prohibited blacks from such places. Angry whites often attacked and burned the buses and beat the Freedom Riders with boards and tire irons. King and other leaders wanted to stop the violence by giving up, but the young students were determined, and willing to face more punishment. As they continued their dangerous journey, federal troops were sent to protect them. Eventually, segregation on interstate buses and at bus stops was outlawed by the federal government.

The next campaign against discrimination was mass demonstrations in Birmingham, Alabama. The goal was to completely fill the Birmingham jails with protestors. After several sit-ins, marches, and other peaceful demonstrations, Dr. King was among those behind bars. There he wrote his famous "Letter from Birmingham Jail." The letter was to all the clergy, black and white, Protestant and Catholic, who had failed to support the crusade. He told them that it was a Christian's responsibility to take action against injustice, and that the tragedy of racial discrimination was not the brutality of the bad but the silence of the good.

Eight days later King was out of jail and helping to organize what would be called "the children's crusade." This march of children and their parents was broken up by police. Children as young as seven were arrested and hauled away in police vans. The next day, over one thousand children and their parents met at a church. Police surrounded the building and sprayed children who tried to escape with powerful streams of water from firehoses, injuring many of them. Then police dogs were released to attack the children. As hundreds were arrested, television cameras showed the violence to the whole world.

Soon thereafter, President John F. Kennedy spoke to America on television and urged Congress to take action on the civil rights problem. But when Congress failed to do anything substantive, civil rights leaders planned a massive march on Washington on August 28, 1963.

Over two-hundred-thousand people, a quarter of them whites, marched on the Lincoln Memorial that day. There Dr. King gave a speech he had not prepared in writing, but suddenly felt within his heart. It would be remembered as his "I have a dream" speech. He repeated the phrase again and again, each time telling of his dream of an America free of injustice and oppression, an America where people are judged by the content of their character, not the color of their skin, an America where all God's children could join hands and sing "Free at last! Free at last! Thank God Almighty, we are free at last!"

The crowd wept with hope and shouted "Amen," but their hopes and prayers were neither quickly nor easily answered. Two weeks later, a bomb exploded in the same church where police had attacked the children's meeting. Four little girls died in the explosion.

Two months after that, on November 22, 1963, President Kennedy, the first president since Lincoln to take positive action to help blacks, was shot in Dallas, Texas. Fortunately, his successor, Lyndon Baines Johnson, was equally concerned about the civil rights of minorities. When civil rights demonstrators began a march from Selma to Montgomery, Alabama, in 1965, President Johnson sent troops to stop the violence being perpetrated by Alabama state police. He also pushed several civil rights bills through Congress, including the Voting Rights Act of 1965 that allowed blacks to vote without paying special fees or taking "literacy" tests. For the first time in United States history, blacks could fully participate in American democracy.

In September 1964, Martin Luther King, Jr. was awarded the Nobel Prize for Peace, one of the highest honors in the world. Although he was now recognized as one of the greatest men in history, J. Edgar Hoover, Director of the FBI, called him "the most notorious liar in the country." Millions of prejudiced Americans agreed, but an enormous majority were proud that such a man was an American and that their country was free enough to allow him to fight for what he knew was right.

Events following the Voting Rights Act were reminiscent of events in India two decades earlier. Just as India had erupted in violence after winning its independence, several large cities in the United States were torn by race riots just after blacks had finally won their long-denied civil rights. Entire neighborhoods were ravaged in the "long hot summers" of 1965 and 1967. Americans were shocked and ashamed to see National Guard troops battling rioting blacks in what resembled civil war. Martin Luther King, Jr. was especially pained to see what his nonviolent crusade had wrought.

Just as the lives of Martin Luther King, Jr. and Mahatma Gandhi were strikingly similar, so were their deaths. On April 4, 1968, when Dr. King stepped onto the balcony of his motel room in Memphis, Tennessee, a single rifle shot killed him. He was thirty-nine years old, half the age of Gandhi when he was assassinated. One wonders what Martin Luther King, Jr. might have achieved if he had lived to be seventy-eight.

# FOR
# FURTHER
# READING

There are over four hundred books about or by Mahatma Gandhi, each putting him and his life under a slightly different light.

*Gandhi,* by Geoffry Ashe (New York: Stein and Day, 1968) and *Gandhi,* by Olivia Coolidge (Boston: Houghton Mifflin, 1971) both give complete accounts of his life, from birth to death.

William Shirer's *Gandhi, A Memoir,* (New York: Simon and Schuster, 1979) has lucid descriptions of the author's experiences with Gandhi during his most active years in India. The book provides extensive background information on Indian culture and India.

*Gandhi's Truth,* by Erik Erikson (New York: W.W. Norton, 1969) gives a fascinating psycho-sociological view of Gandhi's life as it relates to the culture of his people.

Ved Mehta's *Mahatma Gandhi and His Apostles* (New York: Viking, 1976) offers a collection of interesting vignettes about Gandhi, India, and Mehta's experiences with both.

There are many books of Gandhi's writings, including:

*All Men Are Brothers* (New York: Columbia University, 1958)

*Gandhi: An Autobiography* (Kansas City: Beacon Press, 1957)

*Gandhi on Non-Violence* (White Plains: New Dimensions, 1965)

*The Essential Gandhi: An Anthology* (New York: Vintage Press, 1963)

*The Words of Gandhi* (New York: Newmarket Press, 1982)

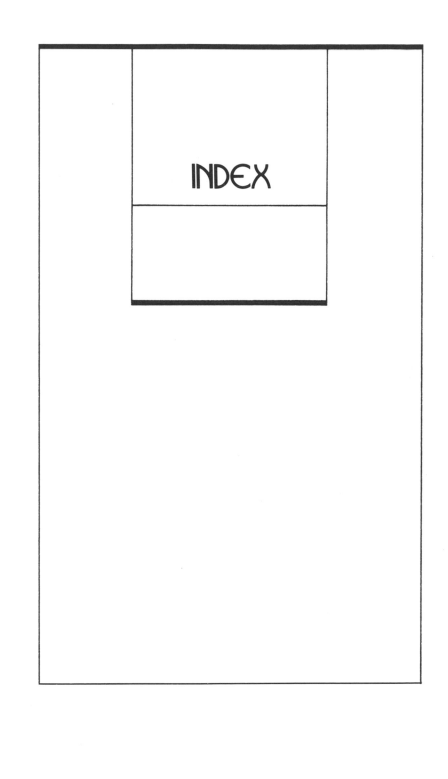

INDEX

Glenn Alan Cheney, a free-lance writer and photographer, graduated from Fairfield University in Connecticut and earned an M.A. degree in that university's School of Corporate and Political Communication. Mr. Cheney, who speaks both Spanish and Portuguese, taught at an English-language school in the province of Belo Horizonte, Brazil. There he developed curriculum materials in technical and literary subjects and gave special classes in English for employees of U.S. and Brazilian firms.

Mr. Cheney is married and lives in New York City. He is the author of *El Salvador*, published by Franklin Watts.